SCOTTISH WEST COAST PILOT

By the same author

Norwegian Cruising Guide
Baltic Southwest Pilot
Frisian Pilot: Den Helder to
the Kiel Canal
Normandy Harbours and Pilotage
Begin Cruising Under Sail

Translations

Practical Yacht Handling

*Other cruising guides published
by Stanford Maritime*

Brittany and Channel Islands
Cruising Guide
by David Jefferson
Cruising French Waterways
by Hugh McKnight

SCOTTISH WEST COAST PILOT

The Mainland and Inner Hebrides
from Troon to Ullapool and the
Summer Isles

Mark Brackenbury

Charts drawn by Alan Wakeman

STANFORD MARITIME · LONDON

Stanford Maritime Limited
Member Company of the George Philip Group
12–14 Long Acre London WC2E 9LP
Editor Phoebe Mason

First published in Great Britain 1981
Revised and reprinted 1982, 1984, 1985
Copyright © Mark Brackenbury 1981, 1982, 1984, 1985, 1986
Reprinted 1986

Charts designed by the author
and drawn by Alan Wakeman
set in 10/11 Times New Roman 327 by Tameside Filmsetting
Limited, Ashton-under-Lyne, Lancashire
Printed in Great Britain by BAS Printers, Limited,
Over Wallop, Hampshire

Photographs of the Cullins, Skye (p. 2–3), Tobermory (p. 79)
and Ullapool (p. 136) are reproduced by courtesy of the
Scottish Tourist Board.

British Library Cataloguing in Publication Data
Brackenbury, Mark
  Scottish West Coast Pilot.
  1. Pilot guides—Scotland
  I. Title
  623.89′29163′37   VK833

ISBN 0-540-07195-1

*For David, who missed it,
but got me there and
brought me back*

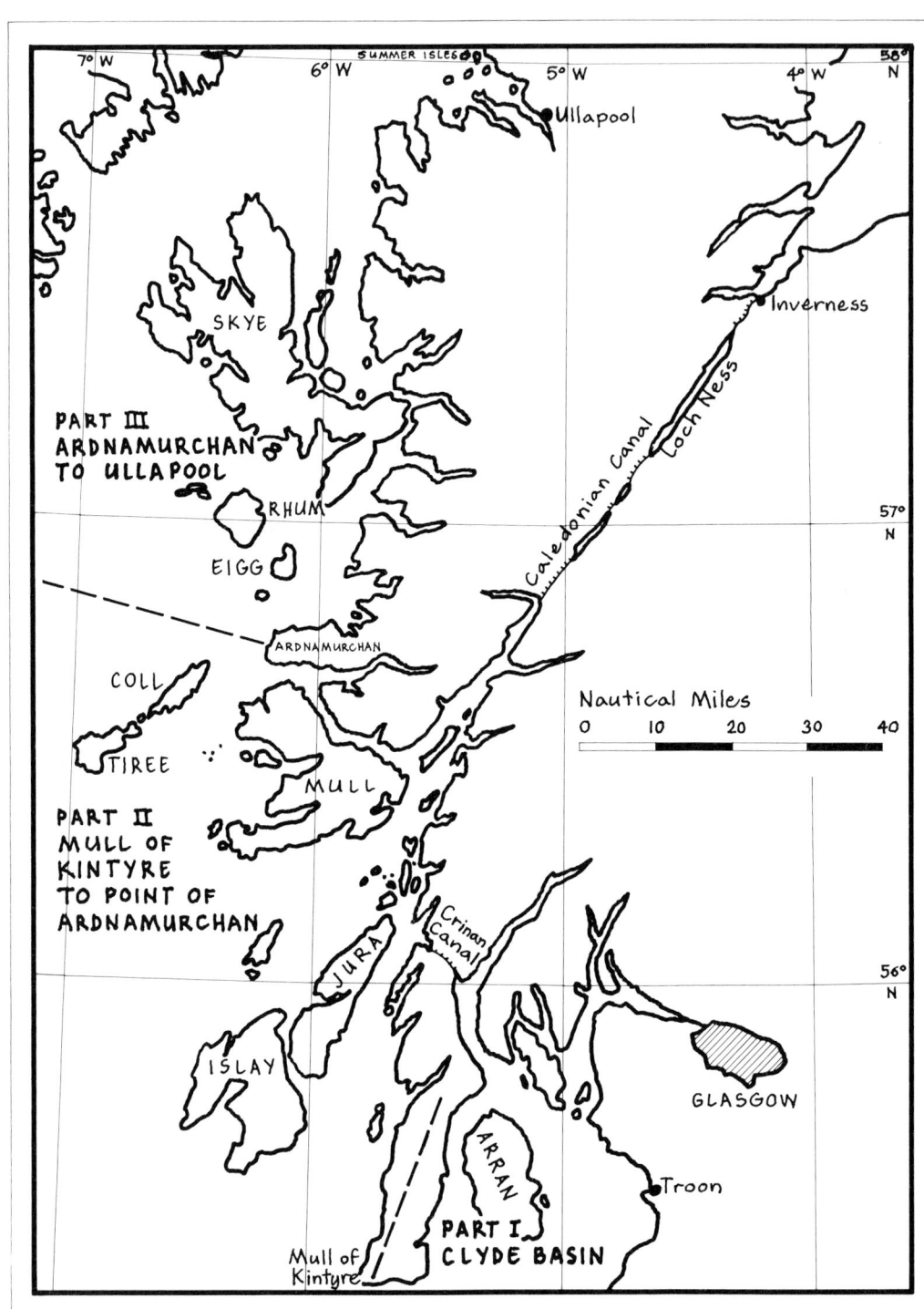

SUMMER ISLES

7° W 6° W 5° W 4° W 58° N

• Ullapool

SKYE

• Inverness

PART III
ARDNAMURCHAN
TO ULLAPOOL

RHUM

Loch Ness

Caledonian Canal

57° N

EIGG

ARDNAMURCHAN

COLL

Nautical Miles

0   10   20   30   40

TIREE

MULL

PART II
MULL OF
KINTYRE
TO POINT OF
ARDNAMURCHAN

Crinan
Canal

JURA

56° N

ISLAY

GLASGOW

ARRAN

• Troon

Mull of
Kintyre

PART I
CLYDE BASIN

Contents

Author's Note

It would be very unlikely, of course, that a part-time sailor would cover the whole area in this book in one season, but I have tried to cover the main area that visitors are likely to want to cruise. If any reader notices new developments, changes, or just plain mistakes, I would be most grateful for a note care of the publishers, Stanford Maritime Ltd, 12–14 Long Acre, London WC2E 9LP. Meantime, I hope the book will help to provide happy and carefree sailing in this extraordinary and beautiful cruising area.

Cruising the Scottish west coast: seals and cows share a pasture in the Small Isles, East Jura.

Cruising in the West of Scotland

This *Pilot* covers the Scottish coast from Troon and the Mull of Kintyre in the south to Ullapool and the Summer Isles in the north. The vast majority of cruising off West Scotland takes place along the coast between these two mainland extremes, and of course among the many islands that lie offshore, sometimes several deep. All of these islands except the Outer Hebrides are covered: to add these would have made the book too long (and probably too expensive) for the average cruising yachtsman, which would have been a pity as only a small proportion of people visiting these waters, or chartering in them, have the time to visit those remote islands. Their waters are so complex that they could easily support a book of their own: perhaps this may be possible in the future.

As the gull flies, it is about 170 nautical miles from Troon to the Summer Isles, so on a straightforward coast like that of the east coast of England north of the Wash, for instance, one might be able to cover every nook and cranny in a cruise lasting a fortnight or so. But here, the deep indentations of the lochs on the mainland coast, and the jagged outlines of the larger islands, ensure that one could cruise the area for half a lifetime and still be finding new anchorages and passages. What is the total length of coastline covered by this book I would not care even to guess: all I will say is that as the coast-line of Skye alone stretches for more than three hundred miles, it seems un-likely that the whole area we are looking at has less than three *thousand* miles of coast: longer than the distance from London to Accra. So readers who are thus inclined will be able to find for themselves many anchorages not men-tioned here. I have, however, tried to describe enough on which to base a cruise plan, or to find a haven close by from almost anywhere in the area.

This cruising area falls naturally into three sections, each with a strong individuality of its own. In the order they are dealt with in this book, the first is the Clyde Estuary and its approaches, i.e. the whole basin lying east and north of the Mull of Kintyre. The southern part is dominated by the dramatic mountains of the Isle of Arran, while to the north lie the softer beauties of the Kyles of Bute, Loch Fyne and the lochs of the Clyde. Here yachts are numerous in the season: not so much so that there is often any real problem in finding a berth, but enough to ensure that advice and help if necessary are always readily available. The harbours are all accustomed to yachts, and many have special facilities. A few sailing yachts and many motor cruisers are available for charter in the area, and sheltered water and a snug berth are never far away; while if the cook wants to go on strike dinner ashore can be had in many of the towns and villages where a yacht is likely to find herself.

The huge barrier of the Peninsula of Kintyre marks the boundary between this section and the second: the waters between the Mull of Kintyre and Ardnamurchan Point. The Mull can be rounded in the south, or the Crinan Canal offers an alternative cut through at the north end of Kintyre, but as I will explain later one is a major sea passage and the latter a lengthy and potentially exhausting task, so in practice there seems to be comparatively little traffic between the two areas, with a majority of yachts staying for considerable periods in one region or the other.

This section is bounded to the north by another natural barrier, a less impressive one when looked at on the chart but very real nonetheless. It is Ardnamurchan Point, which is a barrier because of the difficulty of rounding it in heavy weather blowing from between SW and NW. The yachtsman with a deadline for getting home is risking problems if he gets on the wrong side of Ardnamurchan without plenty of time to wait for a good day for rounding it: indeed it is the normal northern limit allowed by many of the charter firms operating in this area.

The region is wilder and much less populated (sixty per cent of the inhabitants of Scotland live in or within thirty miles of Glasgow or Edinburgh), and in a much larger area there are only a handful of developed yacht harbours. The accent of the English spoken ashore changes from that of Clydesdale to the soft lilt of the West Highlands, and the pace of life seems to slow. Once within the area you are again never far from sheltered water, except when on passage to or from the more outlying of the Inner Hebrides (Tiree, in particular, can seem a very long way), but you can be quite far from a diesel hose or even a grocer's shop. The scenery is on a grander scale, and many people would vote this area the most beautiful of all the Scottish waters.

Our final section is the waters to the north of Ardnamurchan Point. Here, to the amazement of the visitor coming north, the scenery becomes grander yet again, the air clearer, and the facilities even fewer and farther between. The vast outline of Skye is visible on a good day from almost anywhere in these waters, and in the south Rhum produces an incredible sense of drama, with several peaks of over 2500 ft crowding onto an island only five miles across. Here there are no yacht harbours, indeed very few harbours of any kind, and the yacht will lie to her anchor every night, often out of sight of human habitation on land or sea, although perhaps with a couple of inquisitive seals circling the boat, or an oystercatcher standing on a nearby rock and fairly trumpeting threats to any of his kind who might be thinking of moving into his territory.

Weather and sailing conditions
It is notorious that the rainfall in Scotland is higher than that in England, but in fact the annual rainfall in the Inner Hebrides and the coastal strip is only exceptionally high along the mainland coast east of Skye. As far as our cruising ground is concerned, the rest is wetter than the east of England but no more so than say Cornwall or Devon. Mean summer temperatures are

lower than in England, but the effect of the Gulf Stream means that water temperatures are higher than in the English Channel or North Sea, particularly in the early part of the season, which is also the time with the greatest chance of good weather. Indeed, in an average summer the west of Scotland often enjoys long stretches of good weather in late May to early July, and in fine weather the slightly lower temperatures are more than compensated for by the longer hours of sunshine; in the Summer Isles in mid-June there is over two hours' more daylight than in London. Altogether, I feel that nobody need be frightened off a cruise to the West Highlands by the spectre of bad weather, although of course individual summers can be awful in west Scotland as they can anywhere in these islands.

In the open sea the average wind strength is a good deal higher than it is in the south because the depressions that cause the wind usually pass north of Scotland, which is therefore nearer the firing line than England. However, the bulk of the waters covered by this book are sheltered by land reasonably close to the westward, which has the effect of cutting down the sea, and often the actual wind force as well. Indeed, in the lochs and sounds the problem is often calms, even when the forecast has warned of strong winds, but as in all mountain countries it is most important to be prepared at all times for squalls, which can be built up without warning by funnelling and other physical effects, often to two or more forces above the general level of the wind. This effect can be felt anywhere close to land but is particularly true of the inner lochs, and it is unwise to venture into some of these without a reliable and powerful engine as the unpredictable alternation of flat calms and violent squalls can make it almost impossible to achieve safe progress under sail alone. In the outer lochs and sounds, however, this problem hardly arises, and I have enjoyed wonderfully exciting sailing in the combination of strong wind and almost flat sea which one can often find there or among the islands.

Access and communications
For the yachtsman who keeps his boat on the south or southeast coast of England, it has to be admitted that getting the boat there is often one of the problems. If holidays are limited this can be solved by split crews, the use of a trailer for smaller boats, or of course by chartering. But in any case the problem must not be exaggerated: in 1979 I logged only 636 miles between West Mersea in Essex and Loch Linnhe via the Caledonian Canal, and in the same season, returning by the west coast, I logged 480 miles from Port Ellen on Islay to Plymouth, the equivalent of just over 600 to Cowes. If you keep your boat at Chichester you are apparently at the Antipodes, and can go either way! But undoubtedly a cruising boat of average crew strength would want a fortnight or so to get there and another to get back, so to have reasonable time to see the area two months looks like a minimum for those starting from the south; or perhaps a late-season cruise to Troon Marina or Ardfern Yacht Centre in Loch Craignish, lay up there, and then cruise Scotland and return the next season. There is nothing much to be said about the passages up the coasts: both can be done in a series of day-sails except for the passage north from Lowestoft or Great Yarmouth, which is really best tackled as an overnight bash straight through to Whitby, or Scarborough in northerlies. Other

books than this provide the necessary details.

Because of the length of the cruise, crew changes may well be needed, so for planning purposes it is worth being aware that fairly small differences in position on the ground can produce very large variations in the time it takes to get to, say, London. Glasgow is only five hours or so from London by train, and far less by air, and it can be reached quickly from almost anywhere in my first cruising section, the Clyde basin. Once west and north of Kintyre, however, a bus or train has to be got from Oban, Fort William or Mallaig. These also go to Glasgow, but take three or four hours, or even longer for Mallaig. Further north still, there is a final railhead at Kyle of Lochalsh, but the three hour trip which this line provides takes you not to Glasgow but to Inverness, 100 miles to the north and many hours further from London. Kyle is only 100 miles north of East Loch Tarbert on Kintyre, but Tarbert to London by ferry and train is about seven hours, while Kyle to London is thirteen or more. The moral is to plan the cruise around any proposed crew changes, and arrange to be somewhere like Troon or Inverkip when they have to be made. I should perhaps mention that there are air services to Glasgow from several of the islands, certainly Islay, Tiree and Skye, and these can provide the quickest travel of all, on the infrequent intervals at which they operate. But seats usually need to be booked well ahead during the holiday season.

Boats and equipment
Any properly seaworthy boat can be sailed to Scotland and cruise there: deep draft, in particular, is seldom a problem. As already mentioned, reliable power is advisable; and for reasons that will soon be clear, reasonably large fuel and water tanks will be a boon, if not positively vital.

The main equipment needed which by modern standards might be considered exceptional is really adequate anchors and cables. The CQR anchor tends to hold very badly in the sort of heavy weed which is often met with, and on my 30ft ketch I always carry a 30lb fisherman anchor, which holds beautifully in weed on sand or stiff mud. It is also better on rock, as long as a tripping line is used (as it *always* should be in this area, on *any* anchor), but useless in soft silty mud. In a gale, anchored in soft holding, I was once able to hold only after shackling a 25lb CQR on two fathoms of chain to the crown of my 35lb CQR, but those were extreme conditions. A good compromise is a Bruce anchor, which holds much better on weed; so does a CQR of 60lb or more, but that would be beyond the powers of many family crews to handle. In any case, a boat cruising these waters should carry at least two anchors of the full recommended weight, and preferably a third of a different pattern, i.e. one especially suited to holding in heavy weed.

Some anchorages are deep, and two anchor cables should be carried each long enough for anchoring in 15m at low water. This may not sound much, but with tidal ranges in the north of up to 6m at springs, well over 60m of cable may have to go over the side: so to leave some for securing 70m is probably a minimum. Nylon warp may well be more satisfactory than chain, as it is so much lighter to get up, but if used I would recommend at least 4 fathoms (8m) of good heavy chain on the anchor first: this will both help to reduce snubbing and avoid chafe if the bottom end of the cable is sawing backwards and for-

A single plant of kelp, held up by the crew, shows the difficulty of getting a proper hold with an anchor in a thick bed of this weed.

wards against rocks. Even so, an anchor weight is a useful accessory, to reduce snubbing in confined shallower anchorages, enabling the boat to ride to a shorter scope.

My own practice in these waters, for what it is worth, is always to keep the fisherman anchor shackled to its short chain and nylon cable, the latter being coiled down under the main boom and secured by ties. The main CQR remains on the boat's permanent chain, and the kedge CQR with its own short chain is stowed unattached to a cable. This gives maximum flexibility and speed. In this case, at least one additional long (at least 60m) warp is needed, as well as the normal mooring warps. It can be taken ashore to a tree or rock, or used for mooring in difficult harbours or locks when the anchor rope would be employed as the second long warp.

I always reckon that the average British yacht tends to carry fenders that are too small, and often too few. For Scotland I would advise two really good-sized fenders as well as three or four smaller ones: you will not go alongside often, but when you do both the quay and the water may be rough, and they will be needed. Otherwise normal equipment will be adequate, but I would recommend carrying a sextant – even a cheap plastic one – as these waters are ideal for getting accurate fixes by the Distance Off by Vertical Angle method. (Readers who have not met this will find it clearly explained in *Reed's Almanac* and elsewhere: a really accurate fix can be obtained by crossing two such distance-off arcs, the whole process taking perhaps three minutes.)

Anchoring technique

A pilot book is not intended to be a treatise on seamanship, but as a considerable number of yachtsmen nowadays learn to cruise in areas where there is no need, or indeed room, to anchor, I feel that for some readers a few notes on this vital subject may not come amiss. Here, therefore, are a few useful maxims.

Always calculate the rise and fall from the present level of tide, and allow at least three times as much cable as the depth will be at high water. I suggest a minimum of 15m in any case, as even in shallow anchorages any less is likely to lead to snubbing. *And note that where I say, for example, 'Anchor in 5m', this means in five metres* **plus** *whatever rise of tide exists at the time of anchoring.*

Always be a pessimist. Anchoring on a lovely still evening, do not just dump the anchor over the side and go below. Unless there is a stiff breeze or strong current, reverse the anchor in and make sure it is holding. I use half power in reverse gear to 'set' the anchor, and then reduce to quarter power: if the boat does not stop going back, and indeed come forward a little with quarter reverse still on, the anchor is not holding. Much better to pull it up and try again than find you have dragged in a force 6 in the middle of a rainy night!

Always motor round and check the depth all round your swinging circle: the wind may change and, for instance, blow you onto the shore after you have anchored in an offshore wind. With 20m of cable out, that will mean you are lying 40m nearer the shore than where you dropped the hook (the length of your boat counterbalances the curve of the cable). If a stern line is taken ashore, this is of course unnecessary, which is why this is often advisable in very confined anchorages.

Always use a tripping line. Instead of buoying it, it can be secured to the anchor cable about 10m up from the anchor, with the lower end made fast to the crown of the anchor. That way you will always be able to haul in enough cable to reach it, and you minimise the risk of someone else fouling it and tripping your anchor. It can be secured along the length of the cable if desired, by only the lightest of stoppings as until they break and the pull comes straight onto the crown the anchor will not trip.

Always take and write down bearings or transits, so that you can check whether the anchor has dragged or not.

Fuel, water and stores

Cruising this area very soon makes one realise how spoiled southern yachtsmen are! On the English south coast, and also the east coast as far north as Lowestoft, practically every harbour and creek seems to have special facilities for yachtsmen and diesel fuel and water can be taken aboard by hose. (My own home port of West Mersea is an exception, but never mind!) In Scotland, as I have already pointed out, these opportunities are rare, and become rarer the further north you travel. There is no reason in the world why this should cause any real problems for the average yacht, but it does require proper planning to avoid sudden crises.

As far as diesel is concerned, I would say that one should try to have a capacity when full of a minimum of thirty hours' motoring. No doubt fast weatherly yachts with keen crews can get away with a lot less, but my figure is given for the average family cruising yacht. If the tanks are much smaller than this I would certainly carry spare fuel in a jerrycan. Then, in the west and north sections, I would advise filling up whenever the opportunity offers: a five gallon top-up may make all the difference in reaching the next fuelling point if conditions turn unfavourable.

Petrol is less of a problem: it has to be fetched from garages anyway, but these are widespread, and of course all of them sell it whereas many do not stock diesel. Even with a big tank, it is as well for the diesel owner to carry a suitable can for fuel, just in case he *does* miscalculate, and of course whatever funnel is needed for filling.

I found no problem at all with water, once I had imposed an absolute rule that anyone going ashore must always take a two gallon jerry can and bring it back full of water. Good water is available almost everywhere, and people are most helpful, and this steady addition to the boat's tanks keeps them going pretty well forever. I usually sail with only one other crew member: with more numerous crews and thus a faster rate of consumption the rule should be amended to one can per couple going ashore, or whatever experience shows is needed. The cans should only be emptied into the tank just before going ashore next time. This means that if the main tank gives out without warning (when *will* they start fitting contents gauges to fuel and water tanks as standard?) there is always a reserve. Of course, wasteful use of water, such as excessive washing, brushing teeth under a running tap, or drinking the stuff neat, should also be discouraged. But when they find they have to hump every gallon, you will soon find the crew become most co-operative!

Radio communications

There are three VHF stations in the area. Clyde Radio and Islay Radio are both remotely controlled from Portpatrick, Skye Radio from Oban, although up to now Oban Radio still has no VHF capability itself. Working channels are: Clyde Radio, 26 (also calling channel); Islay Radio, 25; Skye Radio, 24. Lewis Radio (working channel 26, 0800—1730 Monday to Saturday only); Hebrides Radio, 26 and 27; and Portpatrick Radio (working channel 27) may also be useful from some positions.

Readers should, however, remember that VHF is propagated on a line-of-sight basis, and in a mountainous region like the Highlands there will be many 'dead spots'. VHF is also useful, and indeed much used, in talking to harbour authorities, Coastguards etc. Oban and Lewis are also MF stations.

Using this book

The remaining three sections of the *Pilot* deal successively with the three sections of the cruising area which I have defined above. There is, however, no way of devising a wholly logical system of describing an archipelago, and whatever method I adopted would have produced anomalies. Where there is a reasonably narrow channel, whether a loch or a sound between two islands or an island and the mainland, I have described it in the general north-going direction which I have adopted, taking each port in the order that it would come abeam. The logic of this is that a skipper may well want to know

17

what is the next good stopping place that he will reach, for instance when sailing up the Sound of Mull, and it is easier if he does not have to read through two separate chapters and try to combine them in his head.

In any case, the reader will find that the cruise-planning chart at the beginning of each section shows the position and name of each harbour or anchorage dealt with in the section, and the use of these plans in combination with the Index will, I hope, make it easy to track down whatever information is required with a minimum of delay.

Talking of place names, there are two problems in this part of the world: one is that the spelling of Gaelic names seems never to have been fully standardised, and the other is that many of the names of islands, bays and lochs give only a simple description of their appearance or relative size, and therefore, as in Norway, names recur again and again. As far as spelling goes, I have adopted throughout the spelling used on the latest Admiralty charts. Gaelic scholars may dispute some of these, but the important thing for the navigator is to be sure that his *Pilot* and his chart correspond. Names occurring more than once are indexed under their body of water or the nearest identifiable island, mainland region, or whatever will make it clearest which is referred to. For a glossary and few simple rules of Gaelic pronunciation – most important if one is to ask for or understand advice from locals – refer to the Appendix on the subject. Gaelic is widely spoken on Skye and many of the smaller islands, but of course everyone in the area speaks English – usually with an accuracy and grammatical perfection unknown in the south.

Charts

A list of Admiralty chart numbers is given at the beginning of each of the following sections. It will be seen that the first of these precede a group in parentheses. The charts that are definitely needed are given first; with the plans in this book it should be possible to use all but a few of the smallest harbours, anchorages and passages described with only these. Those who wish to prospect for their own anchorages, short-cuts or passages, however, will need some or all of the others.

British Admiralty chart 2635 will also be found to be very useful for cruise planning: it covers the whole of the west of Scotland on one chart at a scale of 1:464,000, which is ideal for giving the broad picture while still being large enough to show the alternatives clearly.

Moorings

I feel sure that I need not remind the reader that other people's moorings should never be made use of in such a way as to inconvenience them. In crowded English south coast harbours, where there are numerous free moorings, it may sometimes be permissible to leave one's boat unattended on a borrowed mooring for an hour or two, but this should never be done in Scotland except in a real emergency unless someone can be found to confirm that it is all right. Many moorings have large buoys but are too light for a yacht: judge the weight of a mooring by the gauge of the chain it is attached to – if this is thinner than your anchor chain, the mooring is almost certainly too light for you. If the owner arrives, you must be prepared to slip – cheerfully – at any time of day or night. It is not his fault that you are on his buoy.

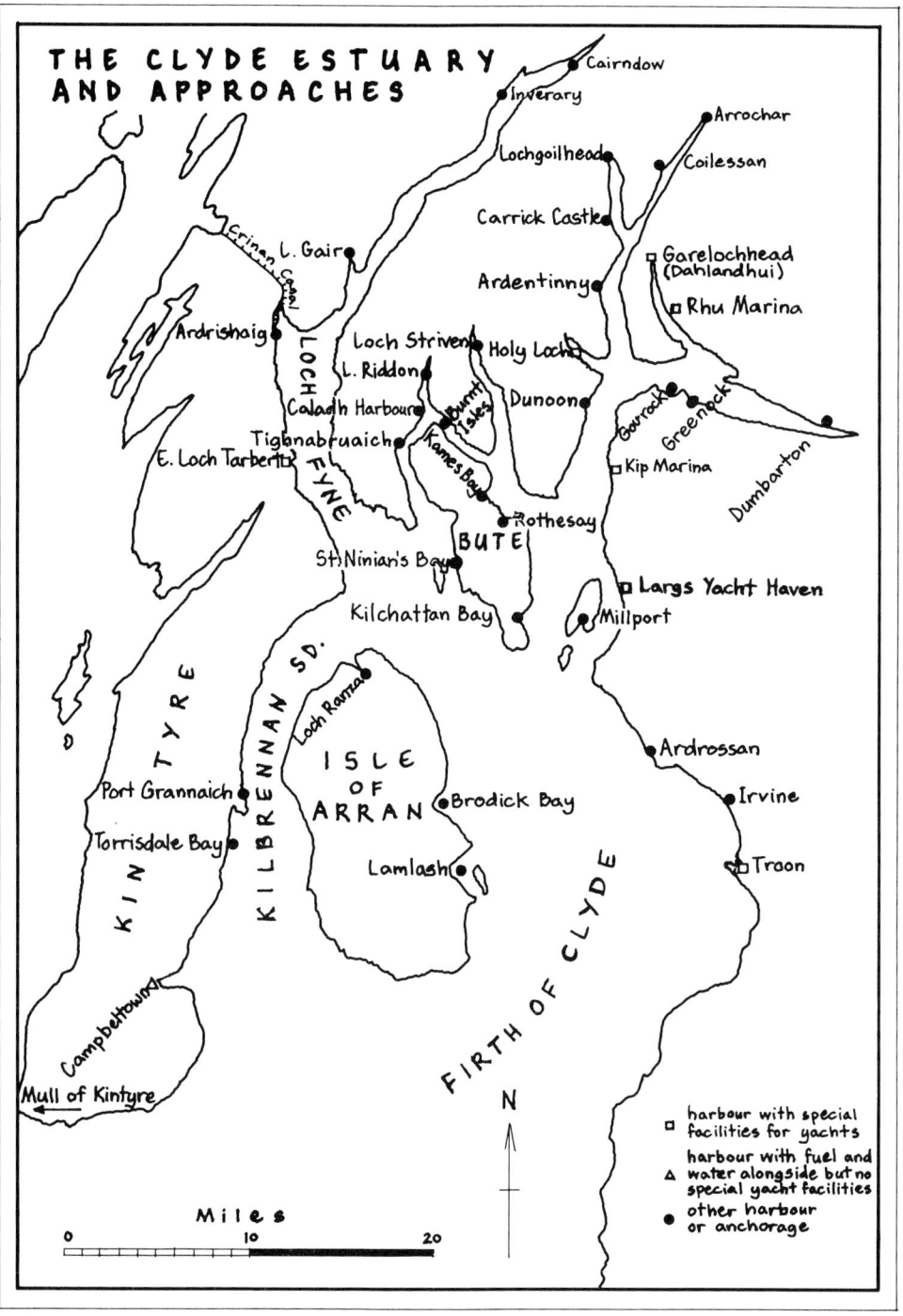

THE CLYDE ESTUARY
AND APPROACHES

Cairndow
Inverary
Arrochar
Lochgoilhead
Coilessan
Carrick Castle
Crinan Canal
L. Gair
Garelochhead
(Dahlandhui)
Ardentinny
Rhu Marina
Ardrishaig
LOCH
Loch Striven
Holy Loch
L. Riddon
Caladh Harbour
Burnt Isles
Dunoon
Gourock
Greenock
Tignabruaich
Kames Bay
E. Loch Tarbert
FYNE
Kip Marina
Dumbarton
Rothesay
BUTE
St. Ninian's Bay
Largs Yacht Haven
Kilchattan Bay
Millport
KILBRENNAN SD.
KINTYRE
Loch Ranza
ISLE
OF
ARRAN
Ardrossan
Port Grannaich
Irvine
Brodick Bay
Torrisdale Bay
Troon
Lamlash
FIRTH OF CLYDE
Campbeltown
Mull of Kintyre
N

□ harbour with special
  facilities for yachts
△ harbour with fuel and
  water alongside but no
  special yacht facilities
● other harbour
  or anchorage

Miles
0   10   20

19

I · The Clyde Estuary and its Approaches

Troon and the Mull of Kintyre to Greenock and Garelochhead

Charts 2126, 2131 (1864, 2220, 2221, 1906, 2381, 2382, 1907, 3746)

1 CAMPBELTOWN TO EAST LOCH TARBERT BY KILBRENNAN SOUND

Campbeltown (see plan) 55° 25½′N, 5° 36′W
Tidal range 2·6m at mean springs, 1·6m at mean neaps
The town lies at the head of a small loch of the same name, partly closed off by Island Davaar. The approach must be made N of the island, which is joined to the mainland by a shoal on its SW side. It is marked by a lighthouse, Fl 20s (obscured from near the shore to the S). The island can be approached on its N side to within 200m: then, by day steer to leave the Millmore beacon (R) 300m to port until the buoys ('A', Fl R 10s, and Millbeg Bank, Fl G 2s) are seen, after which steer between them, pass S of 'B' (Fl G 6s), and then steer straight for the pierheads (2 FG (vert) and 2 FR (vert)) at the top of the bay. At night there are F Y leading lights: by day the rear mark carries a yellow V, and the front one an inverted yellow V. Once well inside the line of the Millmore beacon there are no offshore dangers for yachts, apart from two unlit mooring buoys 2 cables off the SW shore, just NW of the leading line.

Yachts have several berthing alternatives, according to availability of space and inclination. They can lie alongside a fishing boat on the outside of the Old (northern) quay, or (less likely) to one on the inner side SE of the elbow, where there is also water. Shallow draft boats can also dry along the back wall between the quays (2m at MHWS, 1½m at MHWN), or there may be a free mooring opposite the harbour entrance. The best anchorage, though further from town, is in 5m in the bay between the front leading mark and the NATO pier (mud, sand and shell); or less comfortably in 8m off the quarry which can be seen 200m NW of the front mark, mud, but rather steep (do not anchor in less than 8m or you may blow into shoal water) and more subject to wash, and to swell if the wind comes northeasterly.

Facilities include all shops, hotels, restaurants etc. Diesel from the outside of the inner leg of the Old Quay (over 2m at LWS, about halfway between the elbow and the shore). Water from tap on the harbour-facing side of the buildings on the outer leg of the Old Quay, or from a hose by arrangement with the harbour assistant. A pleasant friendly town, and an ideal starting point for a passage round the Mull of Kintyre to the next section of the coast: notes for that passage will be found at the beginning of section II.

Campbeltown Harbour from the SE

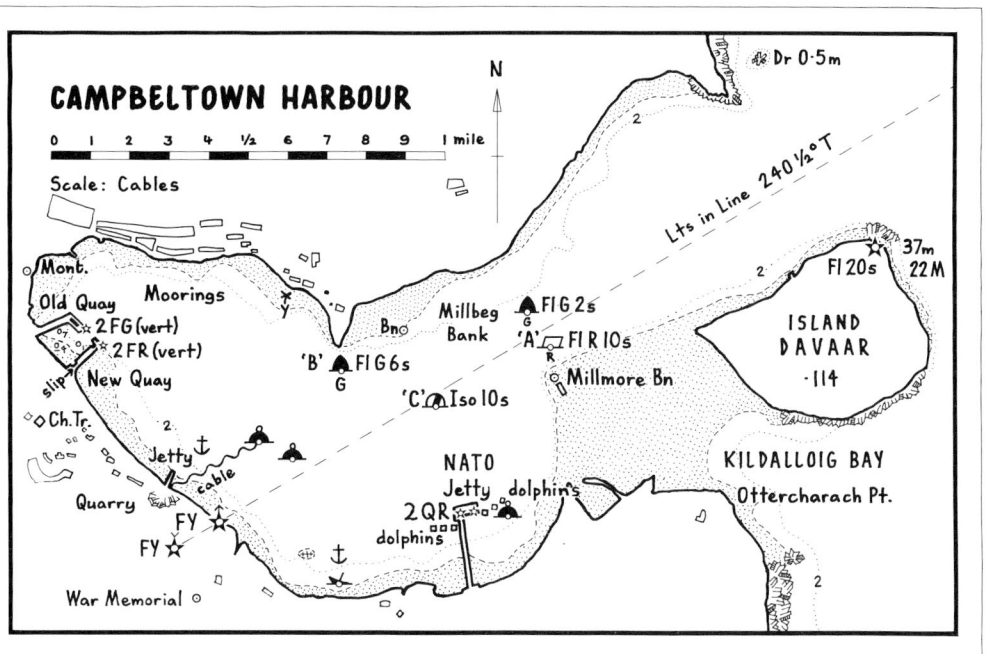

Passage notes: Campbeltown to East Loch Tarbert
The tides run slowly in this area, no more than ½ knot even at springs, and although tide ripples occur off Port Crannaich and Whitefarland Point these are only worth recording because they can look exactly like shoal water and give the navigator a fright! Apart from a spit about a mile N of Cambeltown entrance, clearly marked, all dangers are well inshore.

Torrisdale Bay   55° 34′N, 5° 29′W
A beautiful anchorage 9 miles N of Campbeltown Loch. The bay is just N of a conspicuous white cottage almost down on the shore; anchor in 4m off the castle, which is hard to see among the trees. Some swell in E to SE winds, when Port Crannaich to the N is more comfortable; otherwise very sheltered. Supplies at Carradale, 1½ miles to the N. One of the prettiest anchorages in the area.

Port Crannaich   55° 35½′N, 5° 28′W
A tiny harbour just W of the breakwater (Fl R 10s) E of Carradale village. Least depth 2m alongside at LWS: berth on the quay or alongside a fishing boat as space allows. There is not much room, and I imagine it could be impossible to find a berth in the high season, but Torrisdale Bay is always an alternative except in strong E to SE winds. The harbour is perfectly sheltered, but the approach and entrance are dangerous in strong winds between N and E. Supplies in the village.

Loch Ranza   55° 42½′N, 5° 17′W
Tidal range: 2.6m at mean springs, 1.7m at mean neaps
This pleasant harbour lies at the N end of the Isle of Arran and has spectacular scenery, with 850m peaks within 4 miles to the S. However, in strong southerly winds these mountains send down howling squalls onto the loch, so although the anchorage appears to be perfectly sheltered from that quarter it is wise to use two anchors in such weather as yachts have been known to be blown backwards out of the Loch. Swell in northerly winds.

Coming from the S, the entrance is straightforward as the shore is steep-to until well into the loch. Approaching from the N or E, however, keep land open NE of Newton Point until well across to the S side before turning up the loch, as there is a rocky spit (clearly marked even on chart 2131) projecting offshore from S of the point.

Port Crannaich

Anchor off the castle, which stands on the spit projecting from the S shore, as far in as soundings around the swinging circle permit. Shop, hotel, Post Office. Water tap near the pier at the NW end of the village.

East Loch Tarbert   (see plan)   55° 52′N, 5° 25′W
Tidal range 3·1 m at mean springs, 1·8 m at mean neaps
The most important yachting and charter centre on the W side of the Clyde area; it offers all supplies and considerable facilities.

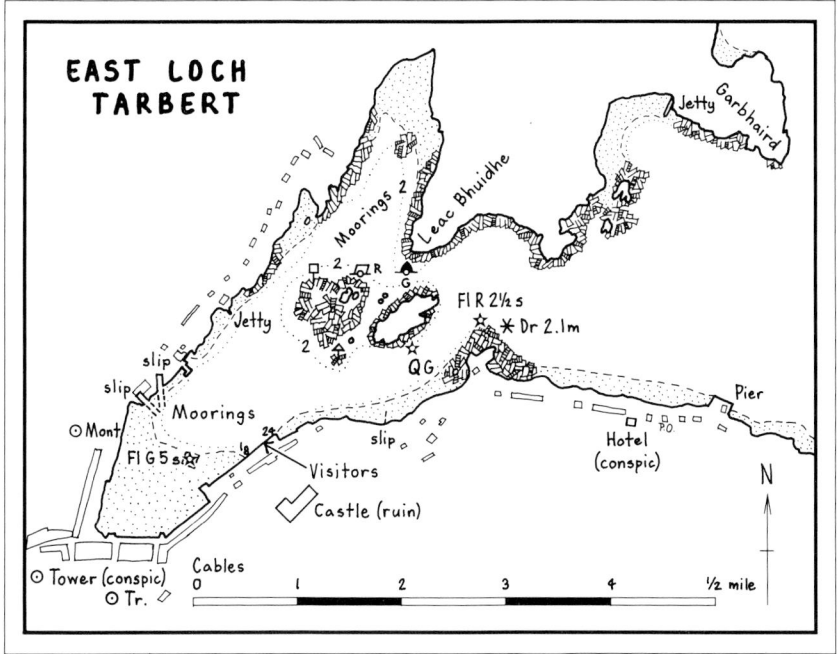

Entrance to East Loch Tarbert

The outer part of the loch is clean, with no offlying dangers. Pass 50m N of the tall beacon (Fl R 2½s) off the S shore, and then turn SW to leave the next beacon (Qk Fl G) close to stbd; then steer about 250° Mag. for the quay.

Most visitors secure alongside the quay, which has about 2m at LWS for the first half of its length though the SW end dries at springs. There are numerous moorings in the harbour, one of which may be free on enquiry. The N part of the harbour is reached by entering midway between Eilean a Choic and Leac Bhuidhe, or from the quay by keeping fairly close along the NW shore of the loch, to avoid the extensive reef S and W of Sgeir Bhuidhe.

Diesel is available by hose at the E end of the quay from John J. Smith. His shop is opposite: if shut try his house through the entry a few yards E of the shop, round the back and up a flight of external stairs, or ring Tarbert 227 which rings in both the shop and at home. Petrol from the garage by can. There is a sailmaker and chandler, W.B. Leitch & Son, on the N side of the harbour. Engineers and repair facilities are available, and when they are not turning over their own boats or dealing with accidents or breakdowns, the charter firms are often most helpful. Stores, hotels, banks etc in the town.

2 EAST LOCH TARBERT TO THE HEAD OF LOCH FYNE

Passage notes
Loch Fyne is one of the better lochs for the sailing man, as in my experience the wind seems to blow reasonably consistently, and without the severe squalls that are found in so many lochs. The average rate of tidal stream is hardly worth bothering about, although it does increase to over a knot in the two narrows. (The Admiralty and I agree on this figure: the rate of 5½ knots sometimes given is greatly exaggerated.)

Before the Otter Spit, the only possible danger to a deep-draft yacht is Big Rock, a mile NNE of Rubha Mhinidhe Beag, which has 2·1m at LAT (2.3m at MLWS). This could cause breaking seas and even damage if a heavy swell were running. Approaching Otter Spit it is important to avoid the drying rock ½ mile off the W shore just N of Liath Eilean: the Otter Spit beacon (Fl G 3s) should be approached on a course between 20° and 50° Mag. to ensure this. Give the beacon a berth of at least a cable. The second narrows looks complicated at first sight, but presents no problems. There is a narrow passage along the W shore passing close to the *westward* of the beacon on the W end of An Oitir (yes, another otter!) – it looks terrifying, but there is masses of water – or a wider one along the E side, keeping well S and E of Eilean Aoghainn and Paddy Rock, the latter marked by an iron beacon tower (Fl W R). N of here the dangers are all close inshore until Inverary, which has a drying rock in the bay to its S, and a spit projecting from the S end of the town. From here all is clear to the head of the loch, which dries for about the last half mile.

Ardrishaig   (see plan)   56° 01′N, 5° 27′W
In the lower part of Loch Gilp, most of which dries. Ardrishaig's main importance is that it marks the SE end of the Crinan Canal, which provides a sheltered route to the Western Isles avoiding the passage round the Mull of

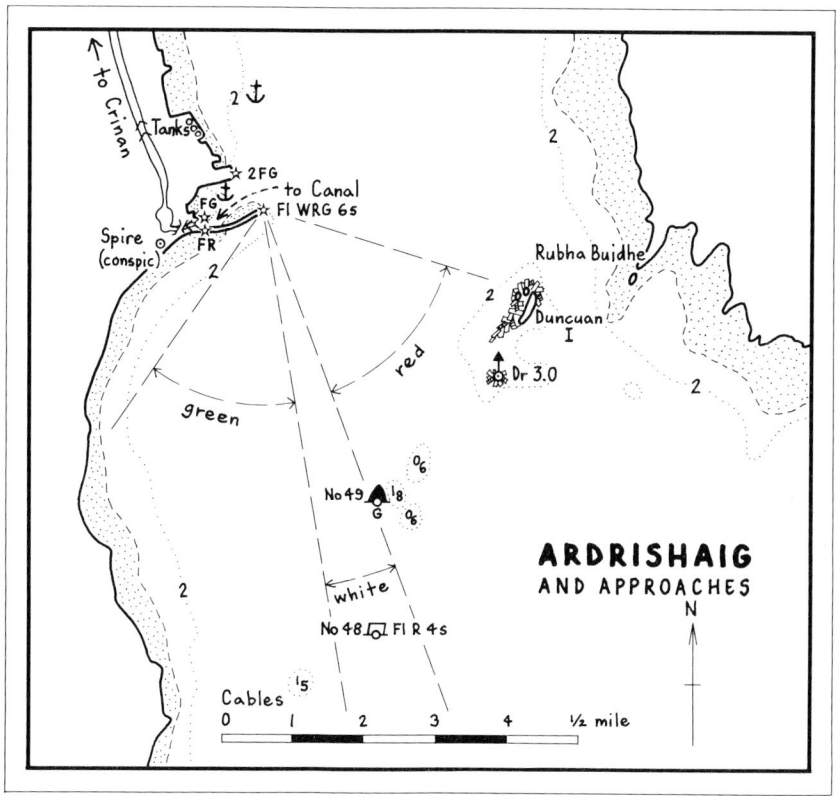

ARDRISHAIG
AND APPROACHES

Kintyre. The canal is dealt with below.

There is a bar almost right across the mouth of the loch, and the entrance is extremely tricky for large vessels. However, apart from a central rock with 0.9m at MLWS, all the hazards W of Duncuan Island have 1.8m or more at MLWS, and are therefore seldom likely to trouble the average yacht. The main channel is marked by a pair of lateral buoys (No. 48, R can Fl R 4s, and No. 49, G conical), and at night the narrow white sector of the light on the breakwater head (Fl WRG 6s) leads in.

The usual anchorage is about a cable NNE of the breakwater head in 4m: beware of going too far N as the head of the loch dries for almost a mile. This anchorage is exposed in SW to SE winds, when it is possible to anchor inside the breakwater just S of the pier, about 25m W of its end. This is out of the main channel into the sea lock. In bad weather it is safer to lock in, or lie inside the lock itself if it has been left open. Water from hose on the S side of the basin inside the lock; shops, hotels etc. Fuel in cans only.

Inverary

The Crinan Canal

An invaluable waterway that enables yachts and other small vessels to avoid the passage round the Mull of Kintyre, which can be very rough in bad weather. It has fifteen locks including the sea locks, both of which can be entered at any state of the tide. There are also three bridges, apart from those associated with locks.

The locks have one or more attendants for each group but users are expected to operate the paddles and gates, and if one boat is passing through alone, the work is very heavy unless there are four or more in the crew. My wife and I went through alone in 1979, so it is possible, but the boat has in that case to be manoeuvred and secured singlehanded, as at least one crew member must be ashore at each lock. The canal is about $7\frac{1}{2}$ (sea) miles long, and the passage can take as much as 6 hours, though if there are crew to spare to go ahead to the next lock and get it ready, then it can be done in $4\frac{1}{2}$ hours or less. Good warps at least 20m long and substantial fenders are needed: there is considerable swirl in the locks when going up.

The locks come in groups: sea lock plus three at Ardrishaig, then a stretch of about $3\frac{1}{2}$ miles (one swing bridge) to the four locks at Cairnbaan which lead into the summit reach. This is about $\frac{1}{2}$ mile long and followed by a group of five locks, and then a final $2\frac{1}{2}$ mile reach with two bridges before the last canal lock and the sea lock at Crinan. The last (i.e. most north westerly) stretch is rock-sided and there are blind corners, so speed should be kept down and the hooter used. It will also be needed at some of the bridges.

Dues are payable at the Ardrishaig end for passages in either direction. Diesel is available alongside just inside the sea lock at Crinan. Typed instructions on the use of the canal are provided at the sea locks on entry.

Loch Gair   56° 04′N, 5° 20′W
This small cove opens on the W shore of Loch Fyne about 3 miles N of Otter Spit. Keep close to the W side of the entrance, which has a conspicuous tower on the point, and then steer to pass close NE of the next point about 250m further in on the W shore before turning N and anchoring in the middle of the cove in about 5m. There is a hotel on the W shore of the cove.

Inverary   56° 14′N, 5° 04′W
Tidal range 3·1m at mean springs, 2·5m at mean neaps
The headquarters of the Clan Campbell and the ancient county town of Argyll, Inverary can be recognised by the conspicuous church tower: the castle itself can hardly be seen until close in.

The shore should be given a good berth until the church is abeam, to avoid the spit which projects nearly 400m from the shore S of the town. Then approach the pier and anchor NNE of it in 4m, mud, or pick up a buoy and enquire ashore: some have been laid for visiting yachts. There is less swell than might be expected in strong SW winds.

There are good shops and hotels. Water tap at public convenience at root of pier, also phone box. There are some plans for development, including the possibility of installing a diesel station, either on the pier or on a pontoon. This may be operating by 1981 if all goes well.

Cairndow   56° 15½′N, 4° 56′W
The best anchorage at the head of Loch Fyne is about a mile beyond Ardkinglas House, charted as conspicuous about 1½ miles before the head of the loch. Anchor in about 10m some ½ mile beyond the point SW of Cairndow, about 150m offshore. Beware of shoals of silt from the Kinglas burn extending ENE from this point. Shop, hotel, P.O.

3 EAST ARRAN, THE KYLES OF BUTE AND LOCH STRIVEN

Passage notes
The Firth of Clyde is too wide to be considered a single waterway, so this section has been inserted to fill in the gaps between the Kilbrannan Sound and the eastern route from Troon up the Clyde. Tidal streams off the E coast of Arran barely exceed ½ knot at springs, but in the Kyles of Bute the streams can approach 2 knots at springs, and up to 3 knots through the narrows at the Burnt Isles. The flood sets up the West Kyle and flows round the N of Bute and down the East Kyle almost to Strone Point before it is stopped by the flood from Rothesay Sound.

The E side of Arran is clean except for Sannox Rock, 2 cables offshore in Sannox Bay. This has 1·5m over it, and the sea breaks nastily on it in E winds. Continuing N, there is no problem W of Inchmarnock as long as the island is given a berth of at least ½ mile to avoid the drying rock halfway up its W side. Inchmarnock Sound, however, has the Shearwater Rock (0·9m) right smack in the middle. Coming from the S this is avoided by keeping Carrick Point just open of Ardscalpsie Point until close in to the latter, after which proceed up the Sound keeping well over to the E side. Coming from the W, steer for the S end of Inchmarnock and round it no more than ¼ mile off. The West Kyle is clean except for a small shoal off Carry Point marked by a red can buoy, Fl R 4s, which can be confusing as by some illusion it appears to be much further E than it is. The navigable half of Loch Riddon has a spit off Eilean Dearg halfway up on the E side: keep well over to the W.

The N end of the East Kyle is complicated by the Burnt Isles (see plan). There are two channels through, both well marked, and the only danger that can arise is from tidal eddies if a boat is trying to sail through in a fluky wind. The rest of the Kyle is straightforward, as is Loch Striven. The latter suffers from violent squalls, has an experimental area which boats must keep clear of, and only one not very good anchorage, so on the whole I wouldn't bother.

Lamlash Harbour (see plan) 55° 32′N, 5° 07′W
Approx. tidal range 2·8m at mean springs, 1·7m at mean neaps
A splendid natural harbour, in which shelter can be had from any weather, though each of the anchorages is exposed to some direction.

At night the harbour can be identified by the powerful Pillar Rock light (Fl (2) 20s); by day Holy Island stands out clearly, being only 1½ miles long and over 1000ft high. Enter by the North or South Channel as convenient, in each case keeping to the Holy Island side of a red buoy. At night it is wise to keep close inshore either on the Arran or Holy Island side once in, to avoid the numerous unlit mooring buoys. The flood runs in at the S entrance (½–1 knot) and out at the N one (½–¾ knot) the ebb in the reverse direction and ½ knot faster.

In winds between NE through N to W or even WSW, the anchorage NE of the moorings off the Lamlash shore is best. Sand and weed, good holding. From WSW to SE, the best shelter is close inshore anywhere for a mile W of Kingscross Point, stiff mud with sand and some weed: I held in a southerly gale there in 1979 on a 30lb fisherman without dragging an inch, and in great comfort. From SE through E to NE, the best anchorage is off the W side of the N end of Holy Island: but note that the owners do not like people to land.

Shops, hotels etc. at Lamlash: land at the jetty. Shop and P.O. at Kingscross: follow the coast road round past the point. Landing can be tricky if there is any swell.

Brodick Bay 55° 35′N, 5° 09′W
Tidal range 2·8m at mean springs, 1·7m at mean neaps
Anchor about 2 cables WNW of the pierhead in 4m, mud; exposed to winds from NNW to ESE. Shelter from N winds can be found S of the castle in 3m, also mud. Very exposed to E winds, and the bay should only be used for overnight stops and in settled weather. Shops, hotels etc in town; water on pier.

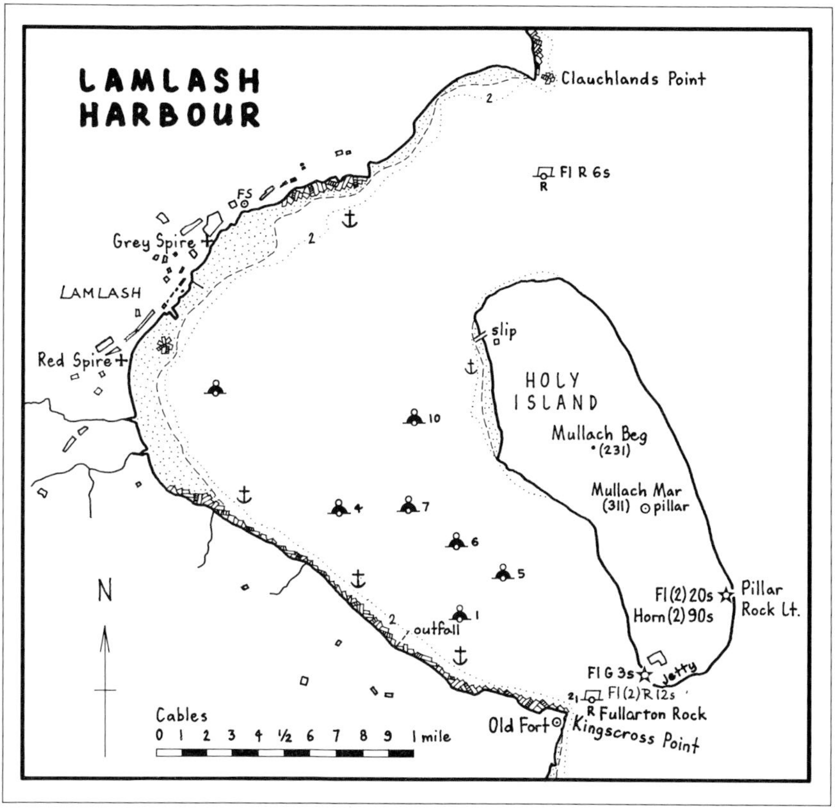

Lamlash, Isle of Arran

St Ninian's Bay, SW Bute   55° 48′N, 5° 08′W
A splendidly sheltered anchorage except in S to SW winds. Approach from
Inchmarnock Sound (see Passage Notes at the beginning of this section) and
anchor 100m E of the black mooring buoy in 6m, mud. No supplies or
facilities.

Tighnabruaich   55° 55′N, 5° 13′W
A famous beauty spot and the destination for many river cruises, but oddly
enough not named on chart 2131. It is, however, in the West Kyle about a
mile NNE of Kames. There is little room to anchor as it is crowded with
moorings, but one of these may be free. If not, anchor to the SW towards
Kames or in Blackfarland Bay on N Bute, ½M NE of Rubha Dubh. This is
sheltered in any weather. Tighnabruaich has all stores, yacht yard, diesel in
cans only.

Caladh Harbour   (see plan) 55° 56′N, 5° 12′W
A perfectly sheltered natural harbour on the W side of the mouth of Loch
Riddon.
    From the S the entrance between the mainland and Eilean Dubh is straight-

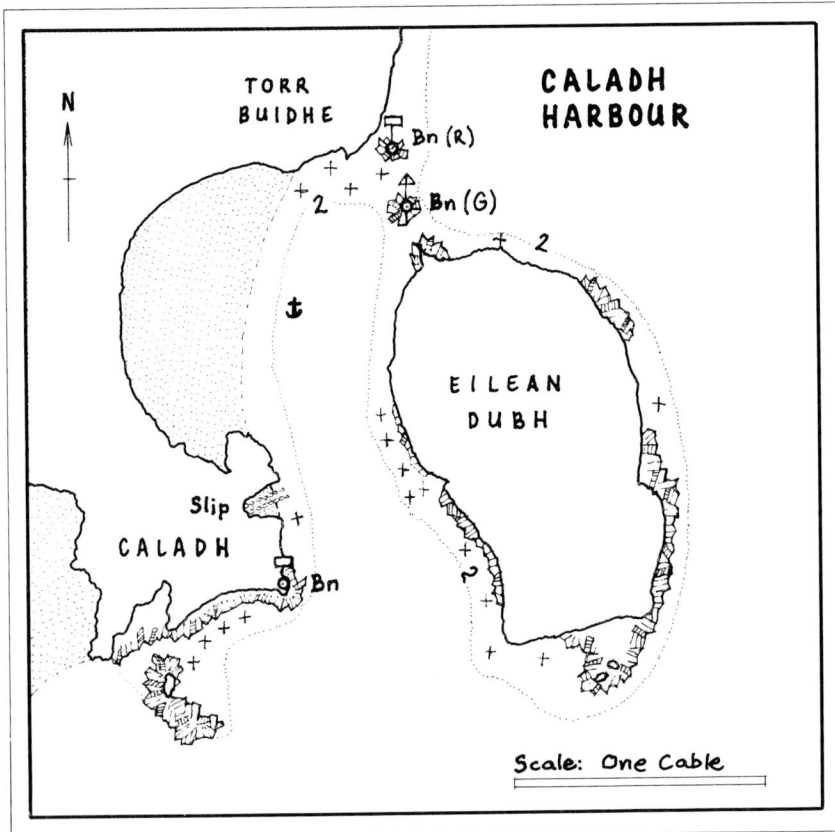

forward: keep midway between the two shores. From the N steer for the conspicuous green beacon N of Eilean Dubh, and leave it close to port on entering. There is a very thin red post to be left to starboard: it is very difficult to spot until close in, but this situation may have been improved by the time this book is published, as it is supposed to have a can topmark. Anchor in 4m about 100m **WSW** of the N point of Eilean Dubh, checking soundings as the W part of the bay dries. Mud bottom. No stores or facilities.

Caladh Harbour: general view looking through from the N.

Caladh Harbour, the N entrance

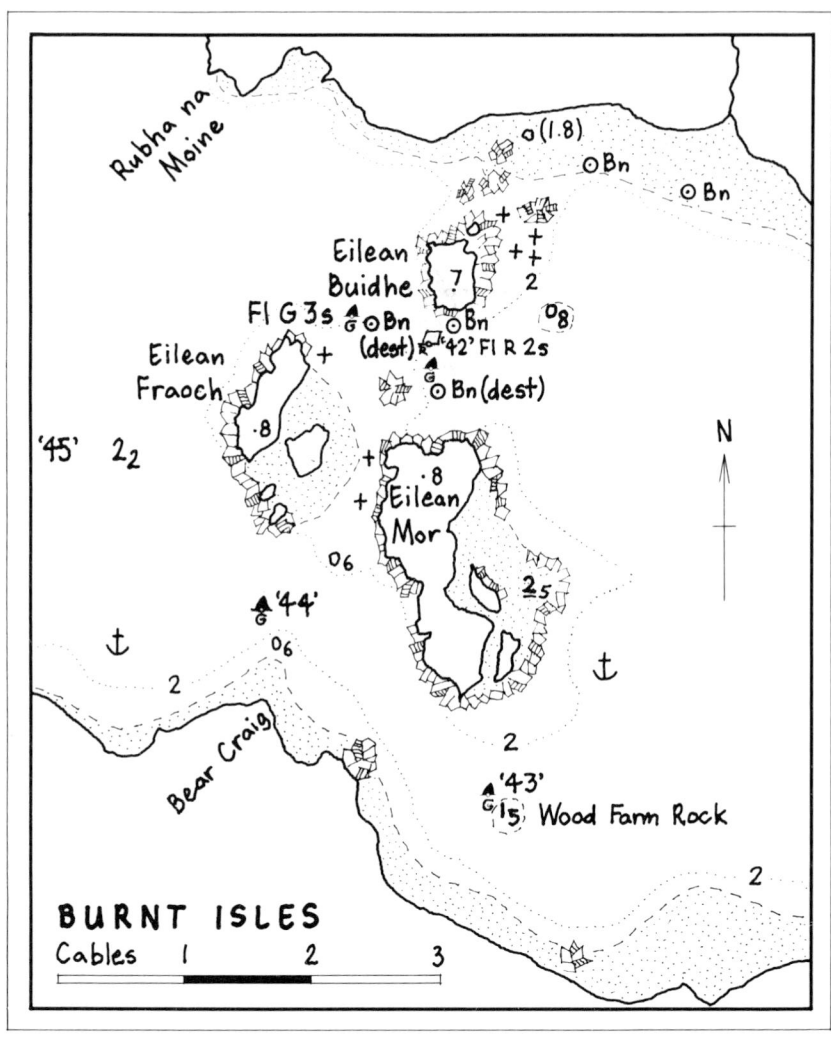

Rubha na Moine

o (1.8)

⊙ Bn

⊙ Bn

Eilean
Buidhe

FI G 3s 🔺⊙ Bn
          G
(dest) 🔺'42' FI R 2s
          A
        🔺 ⊙ Bn (dest)
          G

Eilean
Fraoch

7

2

o8

'45' 2₂

·8

+ Eilean
  Mor

·8

o6

2₅

⚓

🔺'44'
 G

o6

2

Bear Craig

2

⚓

2

🔺'43'
 G (15) Wood Farm Rock

2

N

BURNT ISLES

Cables 1 2 3

Loch Riddon   55° 57′N, 5° 12′W
The loch dries for a full mile at its head, so check soundings carefully. It is
possible to anchor in the bay SE of Eilean Dearg, the islet on the E shore, or
about ½ mile further on the W side of the loch, 8m, mud. Take care to avoid
the 0·7m rock in the centre of the loch, clearly shown on the chart. The
anchorage is as charted, or a little further to the SW. No facilities.

The Burnt Isles, East Kyle   (see plan) 55° 55½′N, 5° 10′W
The N passage is the one normally used when passing through this area, and
as the photograph shows it is clearly and indeed generously marked. The S
channel presents no great difficulty either, but it is important to give a good
berth to Buttock Point to the W, and even more to Rubha Bodach to the E,

The Burnt Isles, North Channel

as this is shoal for up to 200m offshore. It is possible to anchor about 100m E of the S part of Eilean Mhor (see plan), out of the main tidal stream. In E winds an alternative anchorage is WNW of Bear Craig. No facilities.

Loch Striven 56° 00′N, 5° 07′W
As mentioned in the Passage notes, I would advise against the exploration of this loch as it is subject to exceptionally severe squalls, and has an experimental area which must be avoided as its buoys are sometimes joined by wires so that one must keep well to the E side. However, it is possible to tuck in behind Ardtarig Point, the sharp headland on the E shore some ½ mile before the head of the loch, and anchor in 5–10m, mud. The bottom is rather steep, though, and it can be difficult to find a place where there will be enough water if the wind blows westerly, over the low saddle between Cruach nan Cuilean and Beinn Bhreac. No facilities.

4 TROON TO THE CLYDE, ARROCHAR AND GARELOCHHEAD

Passage notes
There are no tidal streams worth bothering about until the Cumbrae Islands are reached, where the narrowing of the Firth produces spring rates of 1 knot to the W of the islands, and 1½ knots to the E. To the N of here, the rates fall again to little more than ½ knot at springs. In strong winds from S to W the coast is very exposed as far as Farland Head, and it is wise to keep well offshore as heavy seas are caused by the banks which extend 2 miles offshore in Irvine Bay. Further N, Hunterston Sands need a good berth, (though I am assured that rumours that they glow in the dark are unfounded), and Toward Point and the mile or two of coast to its N are very foul. Beyond here there are no offshore problems except the shoal off Ardgartan Point near the head

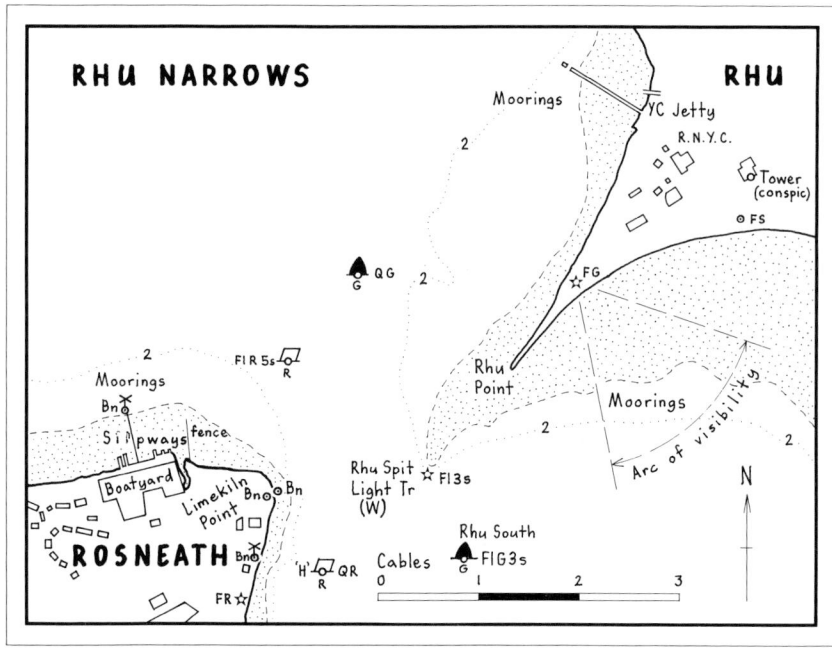

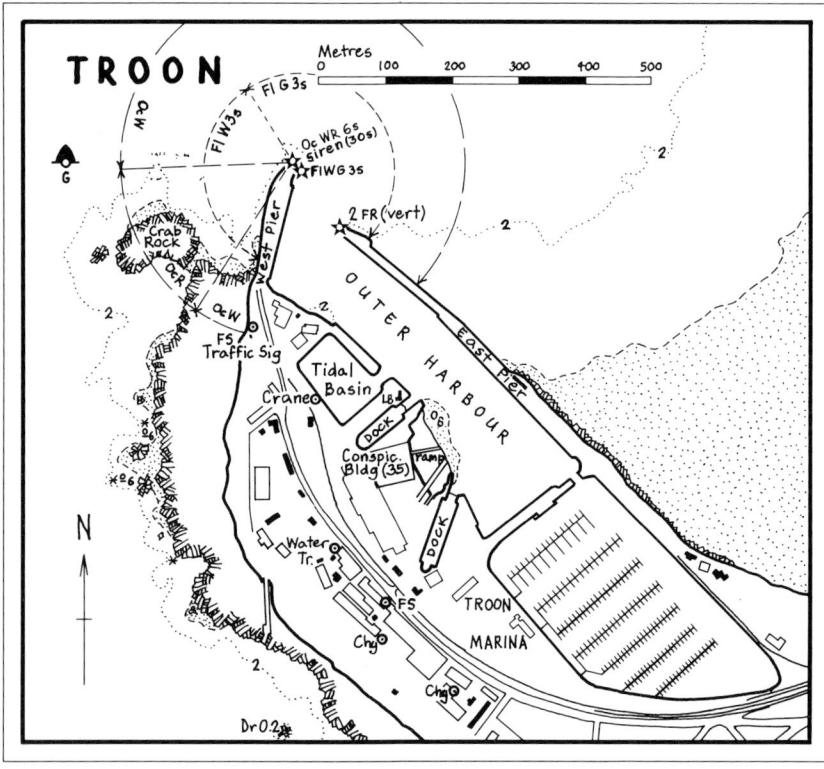

of Loch Long, and the shoals on both sides of the mouth of Gareloch, culminating in the narrows of Rhu (see plan). All the lochs in this section dry at their heads for about ½ mile, but are otherwise clean of hazards except as mentioned above. There are no navigational problems, but heavy traffic may be met and in these confined waters yachts are well advised to keep clear of anything bigger than a fishing boat or small coaster.

Troon (see plan) 55° 33′N, 4° 41′W
Tidal range 2·8m at mean springs, 1·7m at mean neaps
The development of the marina at Troon has made this a major centre for local yachts, and also an important point for repairs, laying up, changing crews, or leaving a boat for a week or two.

In calm weather there are no problems in the approach. Coming from the S Troon Point must be given a berth of at least 2 cables until the green conical buoy marking the end of the spit has been identified: pass close N of this, and steer round the W pier and into the outer harbour. From the N, Lappock Rock is clearly marked by its green beacon tower, and Mill Rock (dries 0·4m), which lies 4 cables NNE of the harbour entrance and is therefore not on the track unless beating S, is marked by a red can buoy to its SW. In heavy weather with an onshore wind, however, it is worth avoiding Troon Rock, a mile W of the entrance, as although it has 5.6m over it the seas break heavily on it. From the N or W, the best line of approach is with the W pierhead in line with the conspicuous gasholder E of the harbour. From the S, either approach from well into Ayr Bay, passing E of Lady Island and steering 10–20° Mag. on the W pierhead; or pass W of Lady Island some 2 cables off, steer 10° Mag. for 1 mile, and then 100° Mag. until the green buoy W of the entrance bears NE, when one can alter course and steer to pass N of the buoy.

The outer harbour is reserved for commercial shipping, but the inner one is now wholly given over to the marina. Pick up a berth as directed or as space allows, and confirm at the marina office. There is a diesel fuelling station, a 12 ton hoist and a 100 ton slip. All repairs can be carried out, although sails have to be sent to Ayr. There is an excellent chandlery combined with a food and drink store (food mainly cans and packets) in the marina, together with

Troon Harbour. The marina is in the nearest basin.

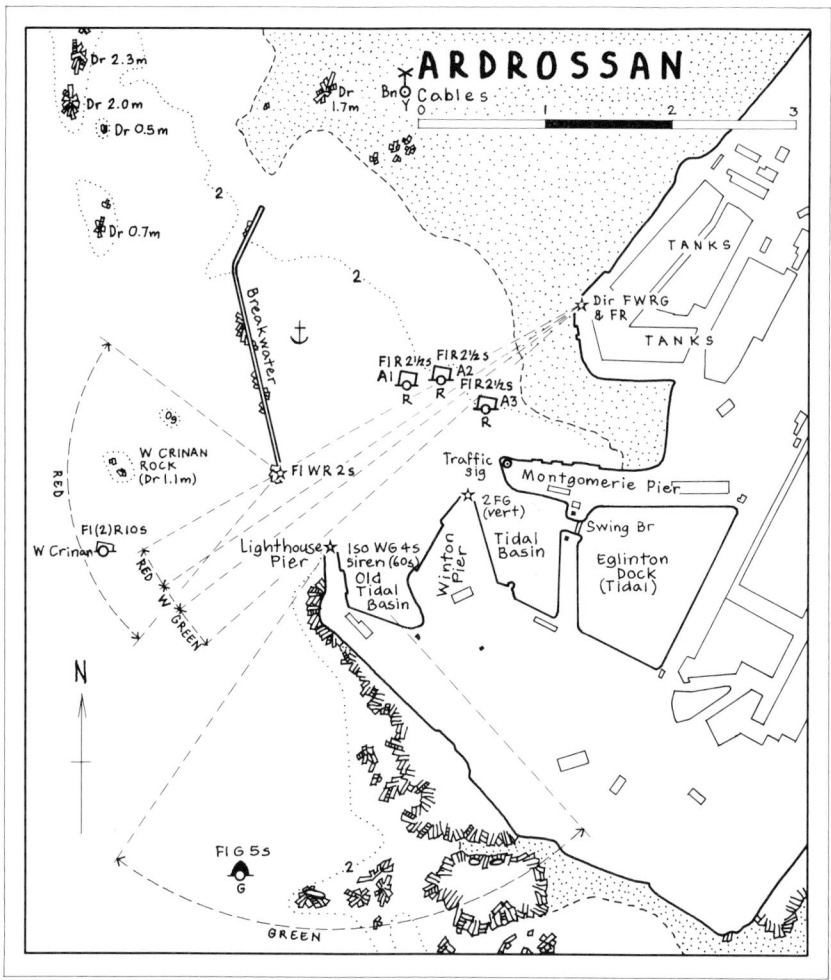

toilets and showers. Other supplies from the town, about $\frac{1}{2}$ mile walk. Communications are excellent, with frequent train services to Glasgow. The harbour keeps a radio watch on Ch 16 from 0800 to midnight.

Troon is a pleasant town, and incidentally I must mention that I had a memorably good meal, with cooking of the highest international standard, in the Auberge de Provence which is one of the several restaurants in the Marine Hotel. Advance booking is advisable (tel Troon (0292) 314444). Be warned, however, that it is a long and rather dull walk from the marina.

This is undoubtedly a well equipped and important marina in the area, for both local boats and visitors. The management is most helpful and friendly (tel. Troon 315553).

Irvine   55° 36′N, 4° 42′W
Tidal range: 2·7m at mean springs, 1·7m at mean neaps
The approach to this harbour is exposed and shoal, with about 1m of water
on the bar at LWOS. In onshore winds it is therefore unwise to attempt the
entry before half-tide, and in SW gales it should be avoided altogether. The
entrance is marked by light towers (Q R to N and Fl(3) G 5s on the S side)
and then by red and green perches until inside the main shoreline. There
are also leading lights, FR and FG, on 051°T. Two black balls by day, or
2 FR (vert) lights by night from the tower on the S shore mean that the port
is closed.

Once inside, one must keep to the starboard (S) side of the channel,
ignoring the River Garnock which forks off to the N, and continue up to the
yacht moorings off the town. Anchoring is now strongly discouraged, and
the visitor must either use a mooring or find a berth for the night on one of the
quays. If in doubt, ring the harbour office (tel 78132). All stores in the town,
water on the quays.

On the whole, I would advise against more than a brief visit, as the harbour
is crowded, and with a first-class marina only 3 miles away the authorities
are not inclined to welcome visiting yachts who have made no arrangements.

Ardrossan   (see plan) 55° 38½′N, 4° 49′W
Tidal range: 2·9m at mean springs, 1·8m at mean neaps
This is a busy commercial harbour and yachts are definitely discouraged, but
it is an important port of refuge, particularly in N or NW gales when it
provides the easiest access of any harbour on this stretch of the coast.

The conspicuous white stone tower on the S end of Horse Island is a good
landmark, but note that reefs extend fully 200m to the southward. Pass
about ¼ mile S of the tower, and steer E, passing S of the red buoy (Fl (2)
R) marking the West Crinan rock and into the entrance between the S end of
the breakwater and Lighthouse Pier. At night, the white sector of the direc-
tional light behind the pierheads leads into the harbour.

In emergency, anchor E of the breakwater, about halfway along its length.
There are patches of sand where the holding is good, but a lot of rock and
stones so it is advisable to buoy the anchor and keep a close watch for signs
of dragging.

Two black balls, or two red lights (vert) at night, on the Montgomerie Pier
(S of the squarish drying N basin) mean that the port is closed.

Millport   (see plan) 55° 45′N, 4° 55′W
Tidal range 2·9m at mean springs, 1·8m at mean neaps
An important yachting centre on the island of Great Cumbrae.

From the S, give the mainland shore a good berth off and N of Little
Brigurd Point. There is also a spit off the NE end of Little Cumbrae with 1·7m
at MLWS, so deep-draft yachts should keep at least 300m offshore between
Meadow and Sheanawally Points. Coming from the W, the extensive spit off
Portachur Point is marked by a S cardinal buoy, but the spit extends E of the
buoy to a line slightly S of it so after passing the buoy the course should be
nothing N of 110° Mag. until the W side of Millport Bay opens up, when it is
safe to alter to steer S and E of the Eileans. From the N via the Largs channel

the coast is clean on the island side, but the tide eddies off Farland Point can be quite sharp at springs and it is wise to give this point a berth of over $\frac{1}{4}$ mile before rounding up into the bay. The harbour itself is approached between The Spoig and the Eileans: at night there is a QG light on a post on the W end of the outer Eilean, and FR leading lights for the harbour.

It is generally possible to tie up alongside the N side of the pier for an hour or two, but the boat should not be left there unattended. The main anchorage is in the bay E of the Eileans. Anchor as far N and W as soundings and permanent moorings allow, sandy bottom. Uncomfortable or worse in SW winds, when an alternative is available just NNW of the long islet with a ruined castle halfway down the E side of Little Cumbrae (no landing or supplies). Millport has good shopping, hotels etc.

Kilchattan Bay   55° 45′N, 5° 01′W

Most of this bay dries, but good anchorage can be found just off the hotel towards the S end of the bay, or a little further SE. Good shelter in winds from the W sector, but the shore is steep-to which can cause problems if the wind changes to an onshore direction, so it is only to be recommended during settled westerly weather. Shops in the village, water from a tap on the pier.

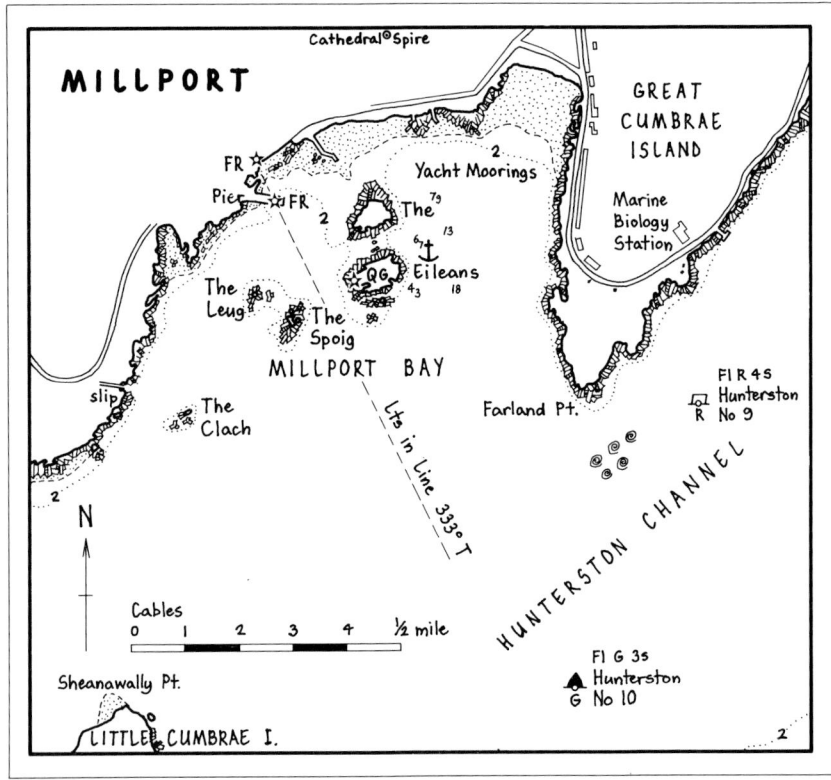

Millport Bay: anchor clear of the permanent moorings.

Kilchattan Bay. Anchor off or SE of the hotel, the tall building in the centre.

Largs Yacht Haven   55° 47′N, 4° 51′W
A major marina constructed inside two breakwaters on the E shore of the Firth of Clyde, E of Great Cumbrae and about a mile S of Largs. A grey stone monument, the Pencil, stands on a point about ⅓ mile N. The area between the South Breakwater and the Nato Pier to the S of it, and in front of the Nato Pier, is prohibited for mooring and all craft must keep clear of manoeuvring ships.

Approach is simple, but as the bottom shoals quickly hold off the breakwaters at least 50m and steer for the red and white mid-channel buoy (Fl 10s) off the entrance, Shallows are marked by red buoys on the N side of the channel. Then steer SE midway between the two white-painted pierheads (lit

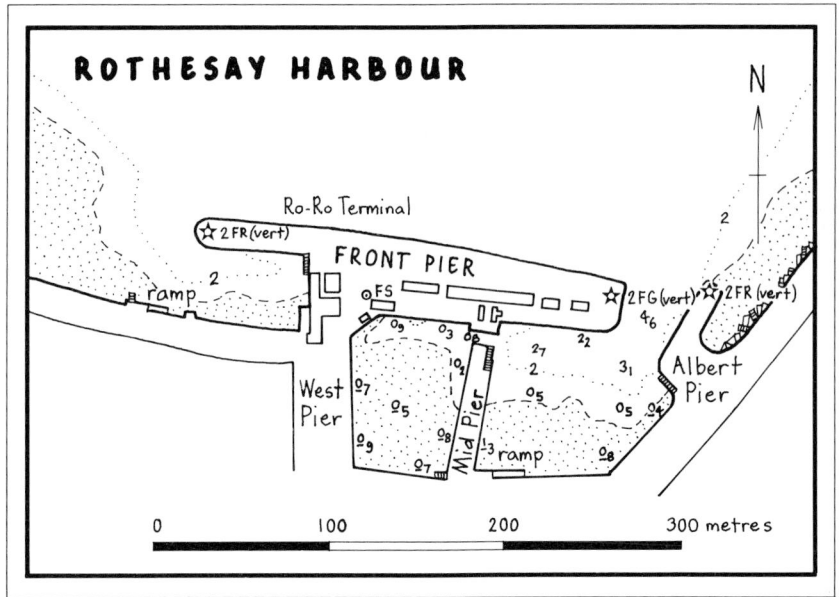

Red Occ to port and Green Occ to stbd). The entrance is dredged to 2m
at LW and orange floats inside mark the shallows.

Ample berths, for up to about 80ft and 11ft draft. Petrol, diesel, water
alongside; yacht charter; hoist up to 50 short tons. Launching slip, hard
standing for layup, chandler. All engine, hull and electrical work; sail repair
depot. Marina office tel. Largs 675333, VHF Ch M.

Largs has train, ferry and bus connections, hotels, shops etc.

Rothesay   (see plan)   55° 50½′N, 5° 03′W
Tidal range 3·0m at mean springs, 1·9m at mean neaps
One of the few harbours in W Scotland where yachts can lie alongside, and a
good place for engine repairs as you are not paying for expensive time used in
rowing out to the boat.

Coming from the N, a course just to the left (E) of the conspicuous ferry
terminal and the church steeple leads into the harbour entrance (see photo).
Enter and moor to the N wall of the outer harbour and report to the HM
(24 hour service). The inner harbour dries, but is more comfortable for yachts
that can take the ground. Fender planks can be borrowed from the HM if
mooring to the outer pilings. Alternatively, there is plenty of room to anchor
between the slipway and the swimming pool N and W of the harbour entrance,
mud and sand. If approaching at night look out for unlit mooring buoys.

Peter McIntyre (Clyde) Ltd have an office on the pier, and will arrange for
engine repairs, etc to be done in the harbour. Their slip and yard is in Kames
Bay (see below). Diesel can be put aboard from a lorry if the quantity justifies;
otherwise in cans. Arrange with Gibson & Co. office on pier. Water from hose.
A major town and resort with first-class shops, hotels, restaurants etc.

Rothesay Harbour. The entrance is just left of the spire. Note the long low ferry terminal building to the right of the picture.

Kip Marina entrance

Kames Bay, Port Bannatyne   55° 52′N, 5° 05′W
Tidal ranges as for Rothesay

A clean open bay, well protected from all directions though some swell does get in in strong easterlies when landing becomes very difficult. Major yard with petrol, diesel, engine and hull repairs including GRP, cranage up to 120ft/ 150 tons, free launching for trailed boats.

The southern shore of the bay is crowded with permanent moorings, one of which may possibly be available: enquire at the yacht yard (Peter McIntyre, tel Rothesay 2311/2719). Otherwise there is plenty of room to anchor up the W side of the bay, roughly along a line between the white house on the N shore

Ardentinny, Loch Long. Anchor just S (left) of the point in 5–10m.

of the bay and the yacht slip to the S. Check soundings with care right round the swinging circle, as the bottom shelves steeply when it does shoal and a change of wind often leaves several unwary yachts stranded. Some shops in Port Bannatyne.

Kip Marina, Inverkip Bay   55° 54½'N, 4° 52'W
Tidal range: 3·0m at mean springs, 1·9m at mean neaps
The entrance lies ½ mile N of a landmark that really does justify the note 'conspic.': a chimney no less than 238m high. From the Kip outer buoy steer E until the rather small channel buoys are identified: there is a minimum of 2½m in the entrance channel at MLWS.

The visitors' berths are by the fuel berth: tie up there and report to reception, which is open 24 hours. Diesel, water, excellent showers, chandlery, repairs and laundry facilities all at the marina; shops in Inverkip, ½ mile away. The marina has 620 berths and the manager tells me that they always manage to find room for visitors somehow. A travel hoist is available; I have no note of its capacity, but it is a big enough one for most purposes.

The surrounding area is not particularly attractive, and perhaps because so many of its users live within a few minutes' drive there is a slight lack of the friendly atmosphere which one finds at Troon, where many more owners seem to sleep aboard. Still, this is an invaluable part of the Clyde's yachting amenities, and a most useful place for changing crews, being little more than six hours from London by public transport.

Dunoon   55° 57'N, 4° 55'W
Tidal range 3·0m at mean springs, 1·9m at mean neaps
The attractive looking bay N of the point with the steamer pier is too shoal to be of any use, and the only anchorage is in West Bay, about halfway along the S shore of the point. The anchorage is exposed to southerly winds, and to some wash from passing traffic. All supplies from the town.

Carrick Castle. The pier with its white notice board is just to the left of the Castle.

Holy Loch   55° 59′N, 4° 54′W

The bottom of this loch is mainly soft mud, and the old anchorage areas are now mainly foul with permanent moorings, so visitors are best advised to arrange to use one themselves. There is a restricted area which takes up most of the loch when submarine movements are in progress: it can be avoided by keeping 2 cables off the S shore to the red can buoy (Fl R 2s), passing close N of this and then steering to pass 100m clear of the Admiralty pier and then Robertsons jetty. The yacht yard, Robertsons of Sandbank, usually has a mooring available for visitors, but best to ring in advance (tel Sandbank (036 985) 383). Do not go more than 100m beyond the line of the jetty without sounding carefully, as the head of the loch dries for a full half mile and the shoals begin to come out from the shore just past the jetty. Water from hose and diesel from drums alongside the jetty, which has about 1½m at half-tide. All repairs; sailmaking sent to John Black of Greenock. They have a small slip where owners can launch from their own trailers for a fee, and a large slip capable of dealing with any normal yacht. This is a good place to leave a yacht for the winter (covered storage available) or for a few weeks. All supplies in Sandbank village.

Loch Long and Loch Goil

Ardentinny, Loch Long   56° 02½′N, 4° 54′W

There is a good anchorage just S of the point with the hotel on it; good holding in 5m, mud.

Carrick Castle, Loch Goil   56° 06½′N, 4° 54′W

Marked as 'Castle (conspic.)' on chart 2131. There is a clear anchorage S of the pier, avoiding a couple of moorings, or N of a line of dinghy buoys N of the pier. Hotel, P.O., shop. Swell in northerly winds.

Lochgoilhead   56° 10′N, 4° 54′W
Tidal range 3·0m at mean springs, 1·9m at mean neaps
The whole head of the loch is crowded with moorings out to the 20m line, so the best bet is to find a free one or risk anchoring with a tripping line on a fisherman anchor. All stores. Beware mooring buoys in the area marked on chart 2131 as 'Experimental', with rafts etc moored nearby: keep well over to the E shore to avoid these. Do not anchor in this vicinity or near Douglas Pier nearby, as the bottom is foul.

Coilessan, Loch Long   56° 10¼′N, 4° 48′W
Anchorage is possible on the W side of the loch, off a prominent house about a mile S of Ardgartan Point; 8m, mud. No supplies.

Arrochar   56° 12′N, 4° 45′W
Tidal range 3·1m at mean springs, 2·0m at mean neaps
Visiting Arrochar, to be sure to keep well off Ardgarten Point, shoal for 2 cables. Anchor N of the pier in 5–6m, mud; or opposite, off the W shore in 7–8m, also mud. Shops, hotels, P.O. etc.

Gourock, River Clyde
There is no room to anchor here. Visitors should pick up a vacant mooring (they lie E of Kempock Point: uncomfortable in NE winds) and confirm ashore at the Royal Gourock YC. Boatyards, sailmaker, all stores.

Rhu Marina, Gareloch   56° 01′N, 4° 46′W
Tide through Rhu Narrows reaches 2 knots at springs. (See plan p34.)
The most convenient stop for yachts visiting Gareloch, with both moorings and alongside berths for craft up to 48ft. Diesel, water, chandlery. Repairs can be done on site, unless the boat is too heavy for the 4½ ton Travelift when they are done at one of the local boatyards. Tel. Rhu 820652. Alternatively, there may be a free mooring in Rosneath Bay W of Castle Point. The Royal Northern & Clyde YC is a short walk from the marina.

Garelochhead   56° 04½′N, 4° 50′W
Tidal range 3.1m at mean springs, 1·9m at mean neaps
Proceeding up Gareloch, boats must keep at least 500ft clear of the submarine base at Faslane, on the E side about 1½ miles from the head of the loch, and at night beware of numerous unlit mooring buoys, most of which lie 1–2 cables from the W shore. At Garelochhead there are numerous moorings, but it is possible to find room to anchor a fair way S of the town on the E side of the loch in 10–12m. All stores, hotels etc in the town, also railway station.

Alternatively, yachts can lie alongside the blue pontoon barge at the end of a catwalk on the W side of the loch. It belongs to the Dahlandhui Boatel, and diesel and water are available by hose. There is always at least 2m water at the outer end of the barge but its inner end dries. The hotel does bar meals.

The Upper Clyde and Dumbarton

Tidal range 4·0m at mean springs, 3·1m at mean neaps

The River Clyde is of course navigable right up as far as Glasgow, but the visiting cruising yachtsman is unlikely to want to sail up a narrow channel in a crowded commercial waterway. Suffice it to say that the channel is dredged to 8m and well buoyed: it begins on the S side of the estuary close in to the Greenock shore. The river is often shoal close outside the channel. Dumbarton lies on the N bank about 7 miles upriver from Greenock; there is a castle on a headland just beyond the entrance to the River Leven. The Leven beacon marks the E side of the entrance: it should be passed on its W side and the buoyed channel followed northeastward. There are moorings and a boatyard.

Readers wishing to pay a visit to this historic town, only 5 miles from Loch Lomond, will have little difficulty in doing so without a chart by following the buoyed channel using the directions above. However, they should arrange a berth in advance with R. McAlister & Son, tel Dumbarton (0389) 62396. The river is shallow where the moorings are, but soft mud and boats of reasonable draft sink in and stay upright. Diesel and water alongside, all stores. The yard is equipped to lift yachts from trailers into the water.

Rhu Point beacon and the moorings to the S.

II · Mull of Kintyre to Ardnamurchan Point

Charts 2798, 2168, 2169, 2171 (2475, 2477, 2481, 2396, 2397, 2326, 2343, 2386, 2387, 1790, 2378, 2379, 2380, 2390, 2617, 2771, 3015, 2652, 2394)
Note: charts 2378, 2379 and 2380 are needed if bound for the Caledonian Canal or cruising Loch Linnhe.

1 THE CLYDE TO ISLAY OR THE SOUND OF JURA

Passage notes
The peninsula of Kintyre is one of the most dramatic geographical features of the British Isles, projecting some 40 miles from the mainland and restricting the width of the channel between Scotland and Ireland to a bare 11 miles. This naturally has a violent effect on the tidal streams, and the whole of the southern end of the peninsula is an area of strong streams, with races, eddies and overfalls. In wind over tide conditions, especially near springs, these can be quite beyond the capacity of an average yacht to handle, so this is a passage which must be taken very seriously.

In calm weather there is of course no problem, although the skipper must always be ready to change his plans if conditions begin to deteriorate. The westbound stream in the region of Sanda Island begins $1\frac{1}{2}$ hr before HW Greenock, and runs for 6 hr. By leaving Campbeltown 2 hr before HW Greenock one will reach Sanda Sound at about HW there, by which time the main force of the stream has begun. The 10 miles to the Mull will be covered in $1\frac{1}{2}$ hr or so, assuming 5 knots through the water, and there will be plenty of north-going tide left to carry the boat well along the Kintyre coast into an area of gentle streams.

In strong SW winds Sanda Sound becomes dangerous, and the best route is to pass $\frac{1}{2}$ mile E of Paterson's Rock (marked by a red bell buoy) which lies a mile E of Sanda; then steer to pass a mile S of the Ship Light on the S of Sanda (a vertical sextant angle will be a great help here); then steer W Mag. until the Mull lighthouse is visible, when it is safe to steer to pass a mile W of that and so up the coast. In these conditions the timing needs to be changed as the full strength of the wind-over-tide effect must be avoided, so departure 4 hr before HW Greenock is best. One is then out of the worst area before the tide has built up to its full rate.

In strong northwesterlies or northerlies Sanda Sound is sheltered and can be used: then the problem becomes the race off the Mull itself. A departure from Campbeltown 1 hr before HW Greenock (i.e. to be off Sanda at HW + 1) will ensure arrival at the Mull after the main force of the north-going stream is spent. Even so, the Mull should be given a berth of 2–3 miles under such conditions.

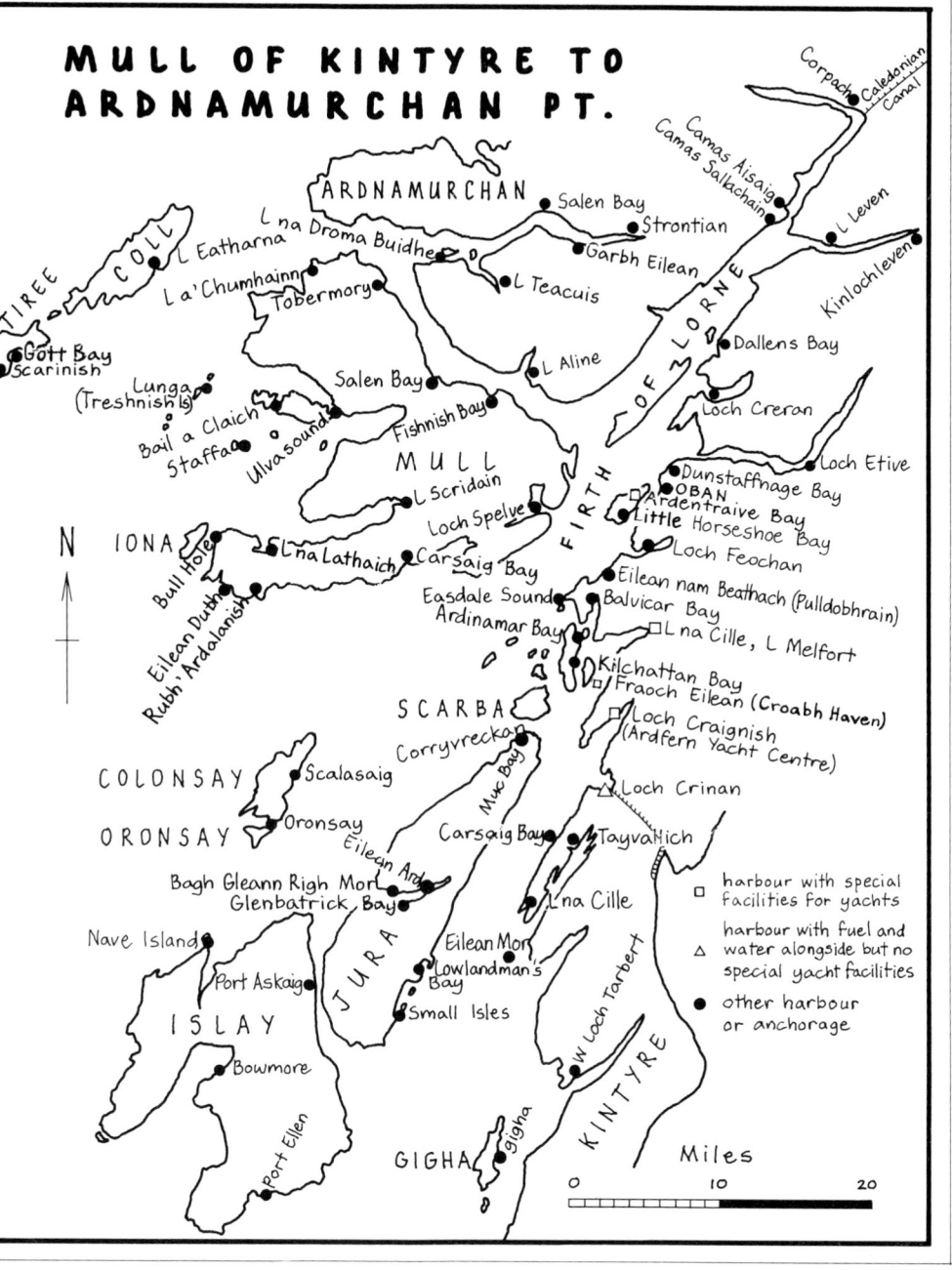

MULL OF KINTYRE TO ARDNAMURCHAN PT.

Corpach
Caledonian Canal
Camas Aisaig
Camas Salachain
L Leven
Kinlochleven

ARDNAMURCHAN
Salen Bay
Strontian
L Eatharna
L na Droma Buidhe
Garbh Eilean
L Teacuis
La'Chumhainn
Tobermory
Dallens Bay
L Aline
FIRTH OF LORNE
Loch Creran
COLL
TIREE
Gott Bay
Scarinish
Lunga (Treshnish Is)
Salen Bay
Fishnish Bay
Bail a Claich
Staffa
Ulva sound
MULL
L Scridain
Loch Etive
Dunstaffnage Bay
OBAN
Ardentraive Bay
Little Horseshoe Bay
Loch Feochan
Loch Spelve
N
IONA
L na Lathaich
Carsaig Bay
Eilean nam Beathach (Pulldobhrain)
Easdale Sound
Balvicar Bay
L na Cille, L Melfort
Bull Hole
Eilean Duth
Rubh'Ardalanish
Ardinamar Bay
Kilchattan Bay
Fraoch Eilean (Croabh Haven)
SCARBA
Loch Craignish
(Ardfern Yacht Centre)
Corryvreckan
Loch Crinan
COLONSAY
Scalasaig
Mue Bay
ORONSAY
Oronsay
Carsaig Bay
Tayvallich
Eilean Ard
Bagh Gleann Righ Mor
Glenbatrick Bay
L na Cille
Nave Island
Eilean Mor
Lowlandman's Bay
Port Askaig
Small Isles
JURA
ISLAY
Bowmore
W Loch Tarbert
KINTYRE
Port Ellen
GIGHA
Gigha

harbour with special facilities for yachts
harbour with fuel and water alongside but no special yacht facilities
other harbour or anchorage

Miles
0   10   20

The Mull of Kintyre, seen from the S.

Strong westerly or southerly winds are almost impossible to cope with in any comfort: if the passage really has to be made the only solution is to keep 2–3 miles off Sanda and then round the Mull 3–4 miles off, reverting to a departure from Campbeltown at 4 hr before HW Greenock (Sanda Island abeam 2½ miles to the N at about HW Greenock–1½).

The south-going passage presents little problem except in the rare event of strong SE winds, when the whole strait is very rough and the best solution is to creep down the Kintyre coast in shelter as far as Rubha Duin Bhain, arriving there 5 hr after HW Greenock; and then steering SW until due W of the Mull before steering SE (or presumably S if under sail) in the hope of getting through the narrows between Scotland and Ireland before the southeasterly stream has built up too far. But except in large yachts I would not advise trying this in more than force 5.

One last word on tide and weather. Races occur in Sanda Sound, S of Sanda, off Sron Uamha (this one is at its worst about 3½ hr after HW Greenock), and off the Mull of Kintyre itself. Any of these will be severe in wind over tide, and the wind is highly unpredictable in this area. Strong southerlies will often appear quite calm right along the S coast of Kintyre, and north-westerlies all the way from Campbeltown to Sron Uamha, where one is met by a sudden blast of wind. So listen to the forecast, and do not be inspired to over-optimism by the fact that local conditions may be calm.

The navigation on the passage is quite straightforward. The various off-shore hazards are never more than ½ mile out, apart from Paterson's Rock described above, and the coast is well supplied with easily recognised land-marks. Once round the Mull a direct course can be set for Islay, or for Gigha and the Sound of Jura.

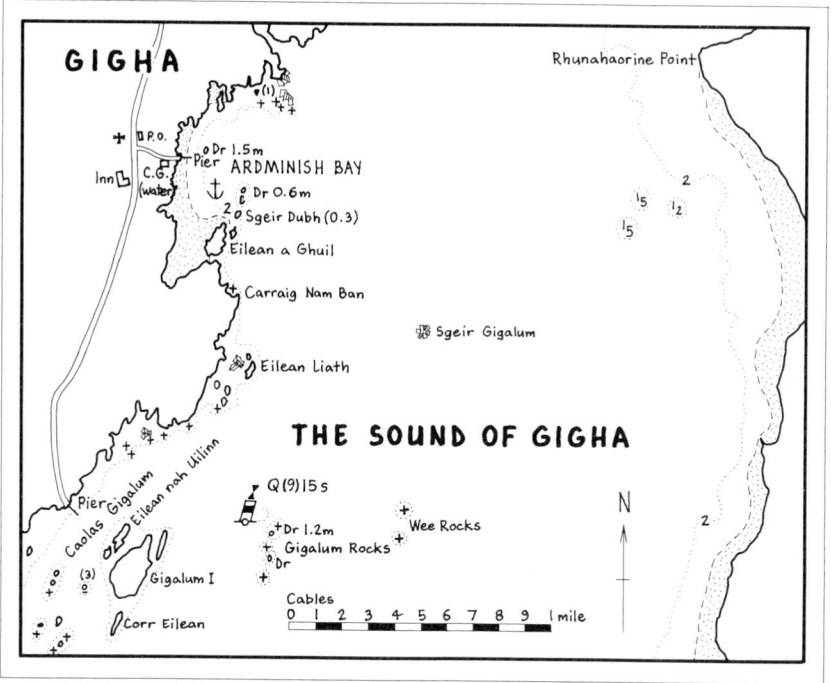

2 GIGHA TO ARDNAMURCHAN POINT BY THE INSHORE ROUTE

Gigha   (see plan)   55° 40½'N, 5° 44'W
Tidal range 0·9m at mean springs, 0·5m at mean neaps
The island of Gigha (pronounced 'gear') provides a sheltered anchorage to
suit any conditions, and the small tidal range enables yachts to creep close in
behind rocks or headlands to get out of the swell. The main anchorage is
Ardminish Bay.

The approach from the S is much easier than the first glance at the chart
may suggest. Both Cara Island and Gigalum (pron 'giggle um') Island are
clean on their E sides, so it is safe to steer for the most easterly visible land of
the group until closer approach makes sense of it, and then steer about a
cable off the E sides of these two islands. Opposite the N of Gigalum a W
cardinal buoy marking Gigalum Rocks (usually dry) will be seen: leave this
close to starboard, then steer to give the main island a berth of 2 cables (there
is a drying rock 1 cable off the islet that is 6 cables N of the buoy) until
Ardminish Bay opens up. Enter the N half of the bay: the best line is to
approach the jetty (at the bottom of the road running down to the shore) on
290° Mag. Once clear of the straight line of islets and rocks visible on the
port hand, turn S and anchor. In SE winds the best shelter is close in to the
line of islets and as far S as possible: in W winds more convenient anchorage
will be found closer to the shore, but keep well into the S half of the bay to
avoid the drying rock 100m off the jetty. Excellent holding in clean sand.

Some yachts prefer to anchor in Druimyeon Bay, but the pilotage is far trickier; as there is little advantage I will leave it for those so minded and carrying chart 2475 to explore. But in strong E or SE winds a useful though isolated alternative is the bay N of West Tarbert Bay, while the latter gives good shelter in its N arm against NE gales, to which all the anchorages on the E side of Gigha are open. Good holding in firm sand, but *only* to be used in settled easterly weather, as both are right open to the W.

Diesel can be got from the pier on the main island NW of Gigalum, but this is exposed and it is often difficult to get alongside. Water in ground floor of the hut at root of jetty (CG on first floor). Phone box and P.O. at the top of the hill; hotel, down to left, has special bath and laundry facilities for yachtsmen. Shops in village further S. A pretty island and well worth a visit.

Passage notes: Gigha to Oban Bay

At HW, when Sgeir Nuadh is covered, the N exit to Gigha Sound is a little tricky. Steer to pass Sgeir Mhor, N of Fank Island, between 1 and 2 cables to the E; and from a position E of this islet, which never covers, steer 100° Mag. until the W cardinal buoy off Badh Rock bears 020° Mag., when course should be altered to pass close W of the buoy. If the buoy is not visible keep on 100° Mag. until soundings have shoaled to 5m (*warning*: the bottom is steep here, so sound continuously and go slowly), and then turn onto 010° Mag. until the buoy is sighted, when it is left close to port. From this position, a course of N Mag. leads out between the islet of Gamhna Gigha and the N end of Gigha itself into clear water.

At lower tides, when Sgeir Nuadh is visible, there are no problems. From Sgeir Mhor pass close E of Nuadh, then close W of the Badh buoy, and then N out into the clear waters of the Sound of Jura.

Proceeding up the Sound, there are rocks off the Point of Knap, the outer

Ardminish Bay, Gigha Island, looking NNE.

one marked by a beacon. On passage, leave MacCormaig Island to starboard, as also Carraig an Daimh, and take care to avoid the long ($\frac{1}{2}$ mile) reef NE of Ruadh Sgeir (Lt Ho Fl 6s). An area of strong tidal streams and ripples begins here: maximum spring rates in Gigha Sound are only 1·3 knots, but in the S of the Sound of Jura this rises to 1·8 knots, and in the Sound of Luing 2·3 knots. These are as it were the main highways: rates in Cuan Sound between Luing and Seil attain 6 knots, while those in the famous Gulf of Corryvreckan run up to $8\frac{1}{2}$ knots or more. Passage notes for these lesser waters appear in the appropriate part of the text below.

The flood stream runs N in these parts, and in strong N winds there are no exits from the Sound of Luing that are not liable to be rough: the best is probably the passage between Fladda and Belnahua, where the spring rate is 'only' 5 knots as against 7 in the shallower passage E of Fladda. Approach as nearly as possible exactly midway between the N tip of Rubha Fiola (the N extension of Lunga) and Eilean Mhic Chiarain (off Luing), and from there steer for the W end of Fladda, curving more W to pass midway between it and Belnahua. In good weather the passage W of Belnahua is perfectly all right as an alternative.

After passing between Belnahua and Fladda, steer nothing W of N Mag. to avoid the reef N of Belnahua. The red buoy marking the Bono Rock will be seen ahead: pass E of this and then steer to pass NW of Easdale and Seil and into the Firth of Lorne. If proceeding N beware the rocks 3 cables WSW of Dubh Sgeir; bound for Oban there are no hazards except a few drying patches around another Dubh Sgeir (the one NE of Insh Island) until the entrance of the Sound of Kerrera (see plan). This is well buoyed and the only traps are the Ferry Rocks, which lie mid-channel and can be left on either side, and Sgeir Rathaid, lying across Oban Bay, on which many an absent-minded skipper has put his boat. Tides in the Firth of Lorne do not exceed 1 knot, and 1·5 knots is the limit in the Sound of Kerrera.

West Loch Tarbert, Kintyre   (see plan)   55° 45′N, 5° 35′W
Tidal range 0·9m at mean springs, 0·5m at mean neaps
Note: the plan only covers the anchorage near the entrance of the loch. To explore the upper reaches chart 2477 will be needed.

The entrance of the loch is marked by the conical shape of Dun Skeig on its S shore. Although not high, this hill is isolated and therefore stands out. Steer just N of its N face. When the entrance is clearly visible, keep well over to the S side until $\frac{1}{2}$ mile past the beacon (QR) marking the extensive shoals S of Eilean Traighe. From here one can steer N and find anchorage in 4m NE of that island. The holding is not very good, in boulders, gravel and weed. No convenient stores. The loch is used by ferries and other commercial traffic, so the anchorage can be disturbed by wash. It is not a lot of use as an overnight port. Pretty to visit, *but on no account* try to explore without the chart mentioned above as there are unmarked shoals.

The Sound of Islay
This sound, between Islay and Jura, cuts through from our northbound inshore route to Ardnamurchan Point to the outer one. The S entrance is very foul on the Jura side, and the streams reach 5 knots at springs, the flood

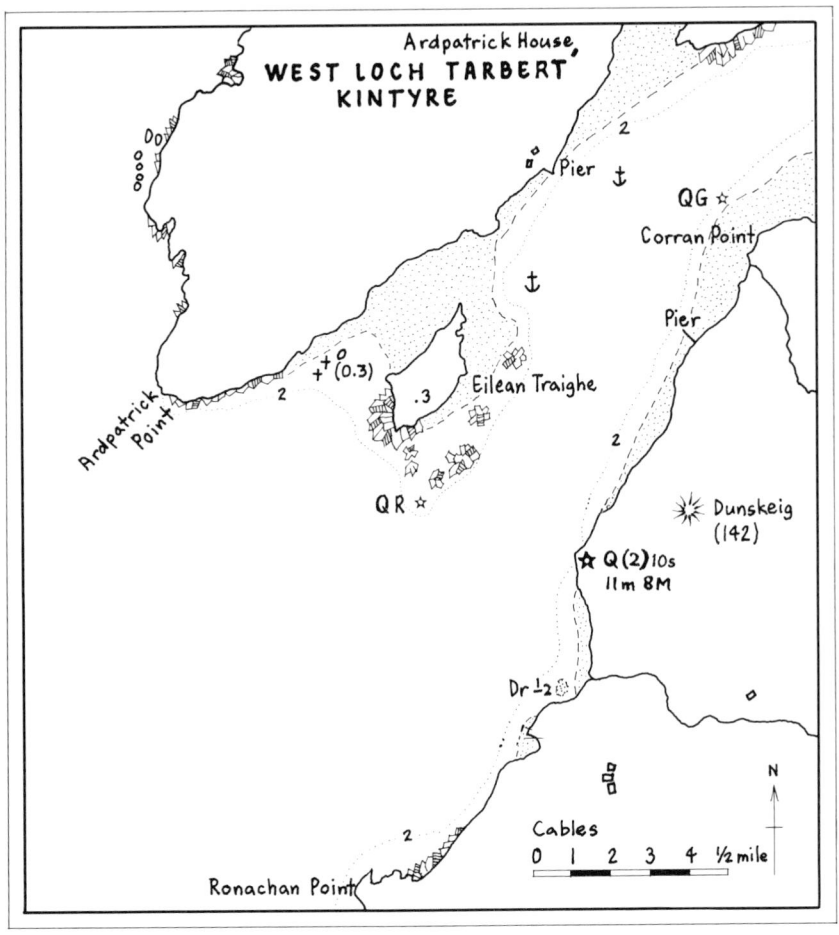

running N in the narrows off Pt Askaig. The N end of the sound is again foul on the Jura side.

Port Askaig   55° 50½′N, 6° 06′W
Tidal range 1·7m at mean springs, 0·5m at mean neaps
This is the best berth in the Sound of Islay. Moor alongside the new pier, very clean with rubber fenders built on. Hotel, shop, P.O., telephone. There is a water hose on the ferry pier, but you have to be nippy to get filled up and off again while the ferry is away. The berth seems to be reasonably sheltered in all winds. It is also possible to anchor off the Caol Ila Distillery ¾ mile to the N: this offers better shelter in strong S winds.

The Small Isles, Jura   55° 50′N, 5° 56′W
Tidal range 0·9m at mean springs, 0·5m at mean neaps
The entrance to this charming anchorage lies between the light beacon on the SW end of Eilean nan Gabhar and a beacon a short distance to the SW,

Yachts alongside Craighouse Pier, Small Isles, Jura.

which marks the NE end of a reef running out from the shore. Once through this gap one may anchor W of Eil nan Gabhar ($3\frac{1}{2}$m, sand with weed patches), or in N winds find better shelter at the N end of Loch na Mile, 5m, mud and weed. Chart 2168 is perfectly adequate for finding these anchorages. It is also possible to tie alongside the Craighouse pier. Shop, hotel, P.O. at Craighouse. Sharp squalls may be experienced in parts of the loch in W winds.

Lowlandman's Bay, Jura   55° 53½′N. 5° 53′W
Tidal range as for Small Isles
This bay is open to the S, although even in S winds some shelter can be found close in to the jetty on the E shore. The holding seems to vary; I found excellent holding in sand and weed, but I have met others who have had difficulty in getting a grip. Certainly the weed is very heavy in places.

No facilities, but with luck you may have a colony of seals for company. Strong squalls can whistle down from the Jura mountains in westerly winds.

Loch Caolisport   55° 54′N, 5° 39′W
In SW winds the swell funnels unpleasantly into this loch, and I would not recommend it as an anchorage.

Eilean Mor, MacCormaig Island   (see plan)   55° 55′N, 5° 44′W
Tidal range as for Small Isles
A most beautiful, wild and strange anchorage, the more so for being in such a relatively civilised part of the area.

From the S, the safest approach is to pass W of Dubh Sgeir and the island, which is clean on its W and NW sides. It is possible to come N between Eilean Mor and Corr Eilean, but there are powerful tide eddies.

Leaving the anchorage in Eilean Mor, MacCormaig Island. The wake shows the correct line of approach.

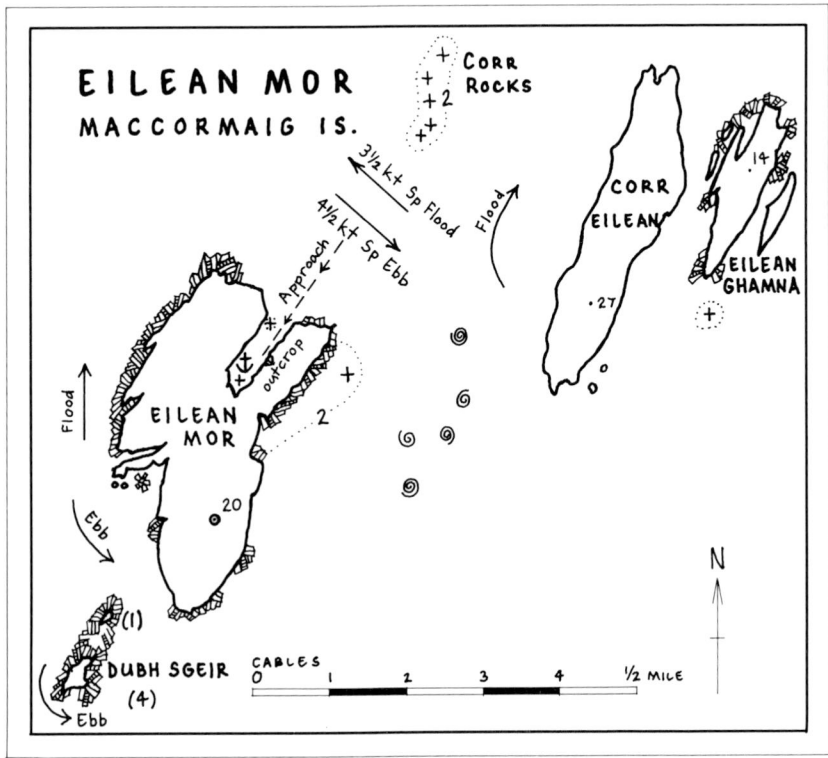

From the N, the problem is to avoid Corr Rocks: if the E end of the island is not allowed to bear W of S Mag., this gives an ample safety margin. Strong streams are to be expected in the area, especially on the ebb.

Enter the inlet keeping one-third of the width from the port (E) side until past an outcrop of white quartz which will be seen on the E bank, then steer for the centre of the pool and anchor in 2½m. The bottom is heavy weed on sand and rock: take a line ashore if expecting a blow. Least depth in the entry channel is just under 2m at LWOS, but the approach is deeper than that until one is well into shelter from any but N or NE winds. This is the only wind direction in which I would not attempt the entrance in over force 4. No supplies: come to think of it, no inhabitants!

Loch Sween   55° 56′N, 5° 41′W
Tidal range 1·5m at mean springs, 0·5m at mean neaps
Chart 2168 covers the S part of this loch adequately, but 2169 (1976 edition) leaves the entire inside of the loch blank: an unpleasant habit which the Hydrographic Department have promised to amend. To explore the loch and its branches 2397 is therefore needed, but readers merely wanting to use the main harbour of Tayvallich can manage with 2169 and the following.

The approach from the S is between Eilean nan Leac (unnamed on 2168, but ½ mile NNW of Flat Rock), and Eilean Ghamhna and its smaller companion, just E of Corr Eilean. From the N, keep out on a line between Carraig an Daimh and Corr Eilean until the loch begins to open up, before steering for the entrance: this avoids Keills and Danna rocks. Once clear of the rocks SE of Rubha nan Marraich, the most southerly point of Danna (the rock furthest out never covers, fortunately), the loch is clean along its NW shore as far as the entrance to Tayvallich, as long as it is given a berth of 1–2 cables and bays are avoided. Sgeirean a Mhain lies right in the middle of the loch

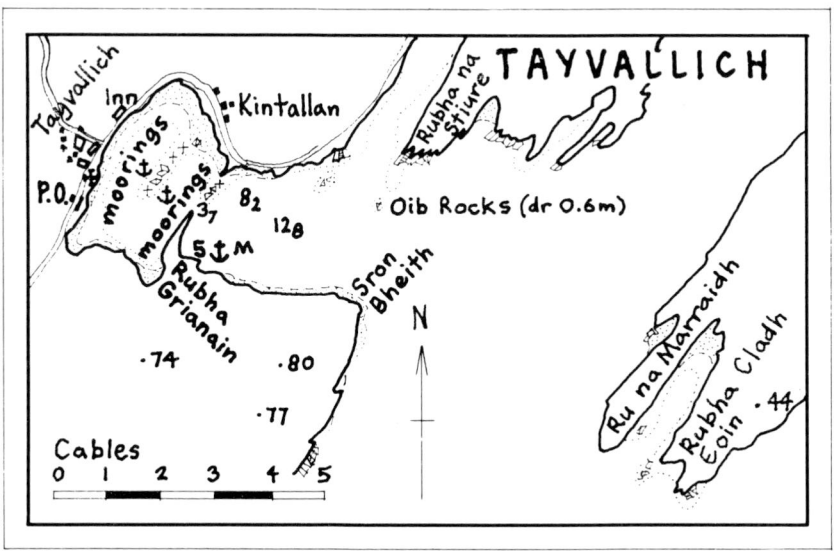

Tayvallich, Loch Sween

just S of Taynish Island: it is only a foot high at HW, so keep a sharp lookout for it. Past Tayvallich, anchorage can be found in several bays at the heads of the loch, notably Port Lunna and the bay SSW of Barr Mor, but for these too chart 2397 must be carried.

Tayvallich   (see plan)   56° 01½′N, 5° 37′W
Most of the inner harbour of Tayvallich is heavily obstructed by moorings, but there is always plenty of room to anchor outside in Loch a Bhealaich in 5–10m, mud, with good shelter. A narrow area 60 or 70m wide along either side of the central reef is also reserved for anchoring, but the outer anchorage of these is 7–8m deep so to be safe it would be necessary to use a stern anchor as well. Shopping is limited, water from a tap outside the P.O./shop. I found the food at the New Tayvallich Inn outstanding, and had a job getting my daughter away from the party that developed after dinner while we were still in any shape to row a dinghy!

Loch na Cille   55° 57′N, 5° 42′W
This loch is somewhat exposed to the SW, but in other conditions it can provide a useful stop when on passage. Coming from the S, keep well off the W shore of Danna until the SE shore of Rubha na Cilleis closes behind the point and approach the point on that line, which clears Keills Rock (1.2m at LWS). The upper ½ mile of the loch dries: anchor about a cable E of the headland which projects S from the N shore with a jetty at its base on the E side. No supplies.

Carsaig Bay   56° 02′N, 5° 38′W
Tidal range 1·6m at mean springs, 0·5m at mean neaps
Except in strong S to SW winds the best anchorage is just inside the S tip of Carsaig Island. Enter the bay and turn N close inside the S point of the island, anchoring when the soundings fall to about 5m. In S or SW winds, better

shelter is found inside the N point of Eilean Traighe, the long island E of Eilean Dubh. Enter this bay midway between the islet and the mainland and anchor about 100m S of the N point of the islet. Do not go in further as the bay shoals, and do not get too close to the point, as it has a rock shelf on its E side. Supplies from Tayvallich, $\frac{1}{2}$ mile SE over the hill.

Loch Crinan   56° 05$\frac{1}{2}$′N, 5° 34′W
Tidal range 1·8m at mean springs, 0·6m at mean neaps
The entrance to this loch is wide and free from hazards, and the only danger as far in as Crinan is Black Rock, 2m high, about 2 cables N of the sea lock, with a companion rock which covers 100m to its E. Anchor clear of the moorings E of Eilean da Mheinn, the island in the bay W of the town, keeping to the mainland side; or in strong northerlies better shelter will be found in Gallanach Bay, the deep inlet on the N shore of the loch between the two pointed headlands. The best anchorage is W of the islet in the middle of this bay in 2$\frac{1}{2}$m. The islet is not shown on chart 2164. All supplies at Crinan, diesel from hose inside sea lock.

Loch Craignish   (see plan)   56° 08′N, 5° 35′W
Tidal range 2·1m at mean springs, 0·7m at mean neaps
This loch contains the Ardfern Yacht Centre, one of the most northerly of all the major yachting developments in the area. As with Loch Sween, chart 2169 leaves the inside of this loch blank, but the yacht centre can be reached using it and the directions below.
    From the S the approach is absolutely straightforward, the main entrance lying between Garbh Reisa and Liath-sgeir Mhor. It is also possible to pass E of Liath-sgeir Mhor, keeping rather to the E of mid-channel until into clear waters near the top of the loch as the W side is foul off Eilean Macaskin, the

Crinan: the entrance to the sea lock for the Canal.

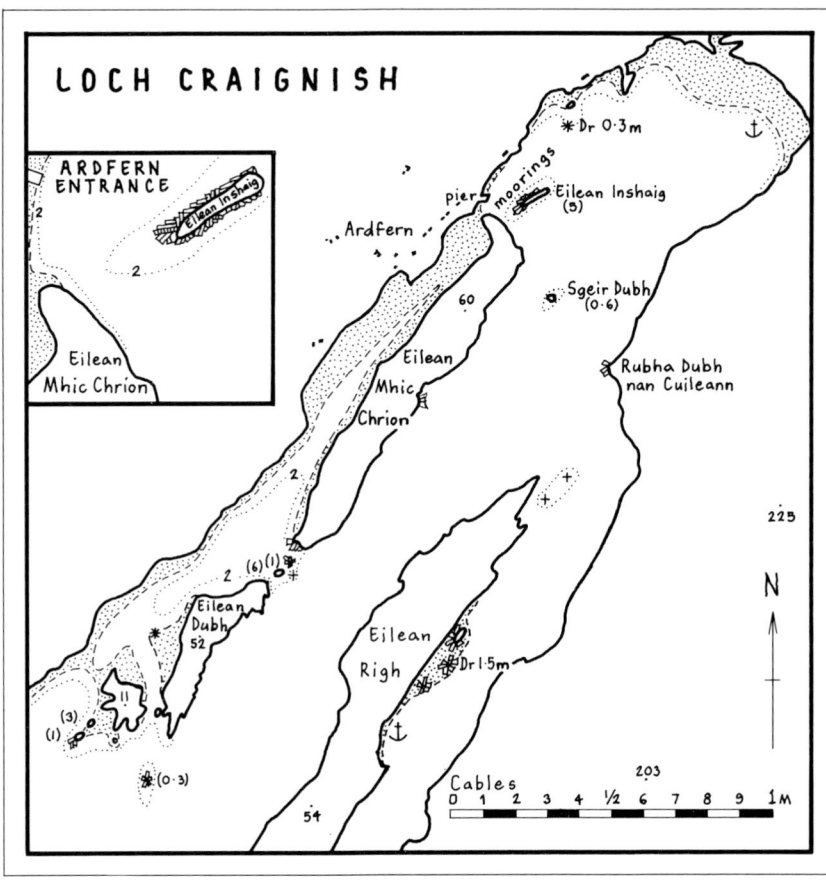

first of the large islands (unnamed on 2169, but marked as 63m high).

From the N, however, the Dorus Mor (the passage between Garbh Reisa and Craignish Point) has to be used unless a wide detour is made, and this is a passage which must be treated with a degree of respect. The flood sets E to W at up to 8 knots, and the ebb the other way at up to 6 knots, the direction changing about 2 hr before HW and LW at Oban (i.e. flood turns to ebb at −2 HW Oban). It is thus vital to avoid at least the full strength of a foul stream, particularly bound for Loch Craignish from the N; and bound N the seas in the Dorus Mor are very severe when the ebb runs against strong winds with a westerly component. If it is necessary to go 'the long way round', the passage between the Garbh Reisa group and the ledge that runs NE from Ruadh Sgeir is not much better, and in bad weather it is necessary to go round S of Ruadh Sgeir.

Once inside Loch Craignish there are no invisible hazards except for a drying rock in the gap between Eilean Dubh and Eilean Mhic Chrion (the islands 52m and 60m high on the NW side): it lies 150m E of the small islet between these two islands.

The Ardfern Yacht Centre's moorings are NW of the islet that lies NE of Eilean Mhic Chrion. Enter between the islands, keeping well over to the Mhic Chrion side: the large-scale chart (2326) is quite wrong in showing the best water in mid-channel. There is now little room to anchor, but there are usually moorings available for visiting yachts: it is also possible to anchor in 5m off the E shore of the loch, exactly E Mag. from Eilean Inshaig (locally Innesaig), the islet NE of Eilean Mhic Chrion. This is more sheltered than the Ardfern moorings in E or NE winds.

Diesel and water are available alongside on the end of the jetty. There is a slip and a Travel Lift; showers at the Galley of Lorne Hotel, which works closely with the yacht centre, in the village. Repairs and chandlery from the yacht centre, run by the suitably Scottish-sounding Carl Stewart, who actually comes from Yorkshire. Telephone nos.: Yacht Centre, Barbreck 247 (636 outside working hours); hotel, Barbreck 284.

The Gulf of Corryvreckan (Coirebhreacain)

This passage between Jura and Scarba has a fearsome reputation, the giant overfalls and eddies which occur there having been exaggerated in sailors' tales into a whirlpool that can suck down a trawler. In fact, in calm weather Corryvreckan is frightening rather than dangerous, as there are no underwater hazards, but with even moderate wind against stream, or even in calm weather if the flood is fighting a swell from the west, the Gulf becomes a mass of breaking seas which could overwhelm a small yacht.

I do not advise anyone to try the passage, but for those who insist on doing so, arrive about half an hour before the slack which is going to turn *against* you. This means that if your are late you are prevented from entering, not sucked helplessly in and through. Streams reach $8\frac{1}{2}$ knots at mean springs, the flood running E to W apart from eddies near the Scarba shore. Slack water is about $1\frac{3}{4}$ hr before Oban HW and LW at springs, 1 hr at neaps. On the flood, it is best to keep well to the S side, passing about 1 cable N of Carraig Mhor and making

Entering Corryvreckan from the E

Entering the Muc Bay anchorage, Corryvreckan, from the N. The beginnings of tide-rips are visible.

good a track due W from there: on the ebb the best water is nearer midstream, but never get N of this as the worst overfalls are off the Scarba shore. Severe overfalls extend as much as 5 miles to the W of the Gulf during a spring flood, and at such times that area must be avoided, for instance by boats on passage from Loch Tarbert on Jura to the Firth of Lorne.

Bagh Gleann nam Muc (Muc Bay), Corryvreckan   56° 08½′N, 5° 43′W
Surprisingly, there is a perfectly good anchorage in a deep bay right in the heart of this dangerous area. The approach is only safe in fine weather, but the anchorage is sheltered in all conditions once it has been reached. From the W, enter early or late on the ebb, passing close S of Eilean Mor and then Eilean Beag. Beware of being set N between the islands: keep an eye out astern and steer as much S of the direct course as is needed to counteract the strong northerly stream. Once S of Eilean Beag, steer SE into the bay and anchor in its S or SE arm, where there is no noticeable stream.

Approaching from the E through the Gulf, at the beginning or preferably towards the end of the flood, the entrance lies between Eilean Beag and the main Jura shore. Keep one-third of its width from the E (Jura) side to avoid a 1½m rock just W of mid-channel, and anchor as before. Even near slack water it is important to be alert and look around constantly, as sudden swirls and eddies can set a yacht a long way off course in a few seconds. **On no account attempt to enter or leave this anchorage more than 30 minutes from slack water at springs, or 1 hour at neaps,** and only use it in *settled* calm weather, as if the wind increases overnight it can be impossible to get away, and one is cut off from all communications. No supplies.

Shuna Cuan and Seil Sounds, Loch Shuna and Loch Melfort
The main route N from the point we have reached is by the Sound of Luing, but on the E of this lies the whole of the above complex, including a cut back onto the main route via Cuan Sound. Tidal streams reach 2 knots (S) on the ebb in Shuna Sound, and as much as six knots (W to E) in Cuan Sound.

Passage notes

From the S, Shuna Sound is clean apart from a few rocks well inshore off the S end of the Luing Island side of the sound. Loch Shuna has numerous hazards, but these are avoided by keeping well over to the W (Shuna) side: if going N from the Fraoch Eilean anchorage pass W of Eilean Creagach to avoid the drying reef that stretches nearly ½ mile S from Rubh a'Chnaip. As far as Balvicar Bay, its useful navigable limit, Seil Sound is straightforward, but this cannot be said of Cuan Sound.

From the S, the first danger is a drying and a sunken rock NE of Torsa: the easiest way to avoid these is to clear the N point of that island, En na h-Eaglaise, by not more than 50m. Otherwise the NE end of the island must be given a berth of at least ½ mile. Once between Torsa and Seil, the next hazard is the reef with patches that do not cover, An Cleiteadh. It lies at the turn up into Cuan Sound; the N end of the reef is marked by a beacon. Pass no more than 50 yards N of this to avoid the rocks off the S point of Seil, and then keep in mid-channel, passing under a 35m power cable and out N of Cuan Point. There is a drying reef 500m WSW of this point, so keep N or W over towards Easdale and into the clear waters of the Firth of Lorne. The flood stream in Cuan Sound (N and W) begins at HW Oban +0415, the ebb at HW Oban −0200; rates up to 6 knots in the narrows at the W end of the sound at springs.

Fraoch Eilean and Croabh Haven   (see plan)   56° 12½′N, 5° 34′W
Tidal range 2·1m at mean springs, 0·7m at mean neaps
A very sheltered yacht harbour and village have been built E of this islet in Loch Shuna. Causeways now link Eilean Buidh on the N with the shore; and connect Eilean an Duin with Froach Eilean (Croabh Is.) and the shore. A stone daymark stands on the hill behind. Approach from the N, passing the green stbd-hand buoy marking a rock off the entrance and the two short breakwaters. Follow the red port-hand marks to avoid a shoal patch and enter the Croabh Haven marina (pron. Creuv-e). The marina (tel. Barbeck 222 and 666) listens on Ch 16 and M. Pontoon berths for craft up to 80ft. Hull and engineering work on site by Camus Marine (tel. Barbeck 225), who also have diesel, water, chandlery, hard standing for winter layup and a hoist for up to 16 short tons displ. and 13ft 6in max. beam.

Kilchattan Bay   56° 13′N, 5° 38′W
Tidal range 2·1m at mean springs, 0·7m at mean neaps
A bay on the W side of Shuna Sound, N of the hamlet of Toberonochy, offering good shelter except in NE winds. Anchor in mud as far in as soundings allow. Some stores, P.O.

Ardinamar Bay   (see plan)   56° 15′N, 5° 37′W
Tidal range 2·2m at mean springs, 0·8m at mean neaps
This tiny lagoon SW of Torsa is tricky to get into, but offers perfect shelter once inside. Approach the white paint-mark on the S headland on a course of W Mag. until within 10m of the shore; then steer for the gap between the

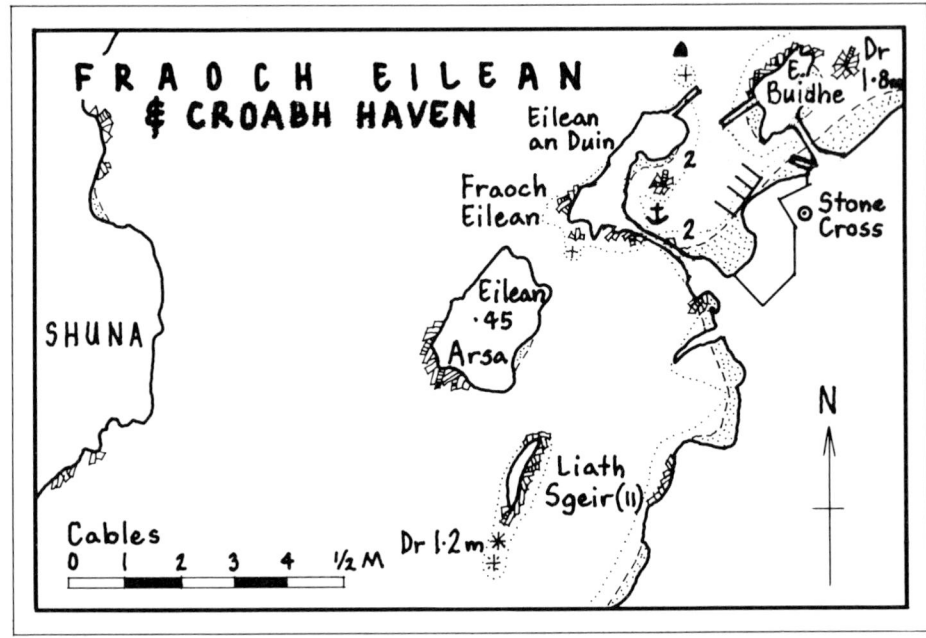

FRAOCH EILEAN & CROABH HAVEN

Eilean an Duin

Fraoch Eilean

E. Buidhe

Dr 1·8ᵐ

2

2

Stone Cross

SHUNA

Eilean Arsa ·45

Liath Sgeir(11)

Cables
0 1 2 3 4 ½M

Dr 1·2m

N

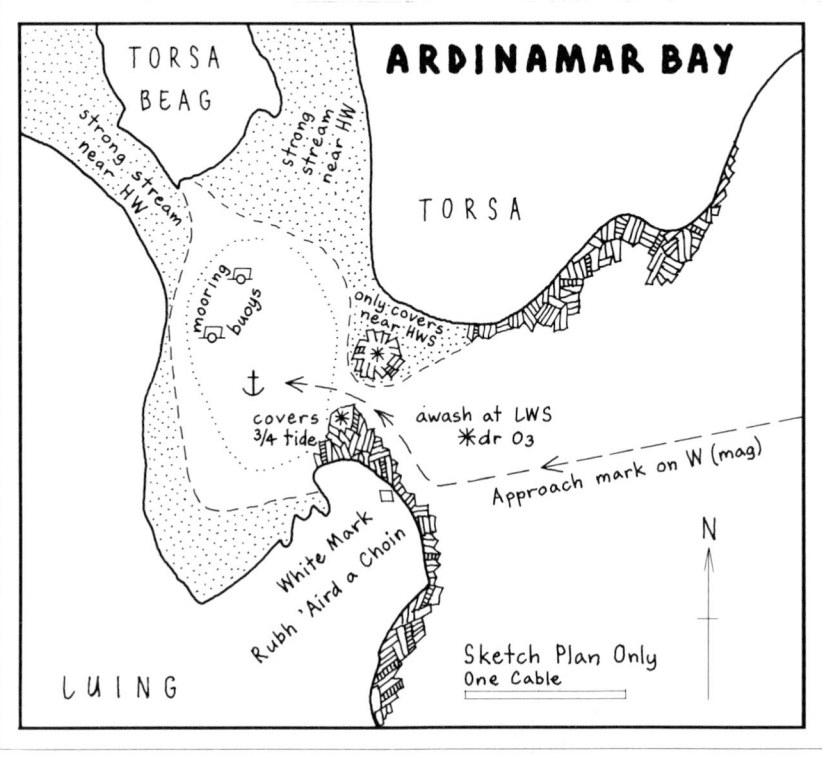

TORSA BEAG

ARDINAMAR BAY

strong stream near HW

strong stream near HW

TORSA

mooring buoys

only covers near HWS

covers ¾ tide

awash at LWS
dr 0₃

Approach mark on W (mag)

White Mark
Rubh 'Aird a Choin

LUING

N

Sketch Plan Only
One Cable

two exposed rocks at the W end of the narrows, so as to pass a quarter of the width of the gap from the more southerly rock. This route carries 1·2m at MLWS: it is possible to find more water by careful exploration, and this is safe except in winds from E to SE, when some swell may get into the entrance. I am told that it is possible to get in at MLWS drawing 2m, and when the tide is low enough for this to be necessary the outer drying rock will be visible, making things easier.

Once inside, anchor in 2m in the middle of the pool or more to the S: the N end is disturbed by strong tidal streams near HW, when the drying creeks through to Cuan Sound cover. No supplies.

Balvicar Bay   56° 17½′N, 5° 36′W
Tidal range 2·3m at mean springs, 0·9m at mean neaps
Chart 2169 leaves the N part of Seil Sound blank, but there are no offshore hazards until the sound begins to open out into a large lagoon (at 17½′N). The anchorage lies W of the islet Eilean Tornal that lies in the S part of the lagoon. Both it and the shore opposite have offlying mudbanks, but a course NW midway between the islet and the Seil shore carries at least 3m at LWS. The anchorage is a cable W of the islet in 4m, mud. Do not go any further N as the N part of the bay dries. This is a charming anchorage, totally quiet in all winds. P.O./store, also frequent food vans. Water from a tap on the road from the jetty S of the anchorage to the village.

Loch na Cille, Loch Melfort   56° 15½′N, 5° 29′W
Loch Melfort is perfectly clear as long as it is navigated well over to its S side. Loch na Cille (pron. 'na Keel') is the extreme E extension, and is the headquarters of Camus Marine, a major boatyard. They have moorings and there is room to anchor, but when approaching beware of a dry-ing reef extending 200m from the NE shore, marked by a perch. There is also a rock, unmarked on even the large-scale chart, near the S shore. It has about ½m over it at LWOS and is marked by a black and white perch with triangle topmark, and it is difficult to see because it is right in among the moorings. Do not attempt to pass between this perch and the shore to the S, as it is mostly shoal.

Entering Easdale Sound from the N

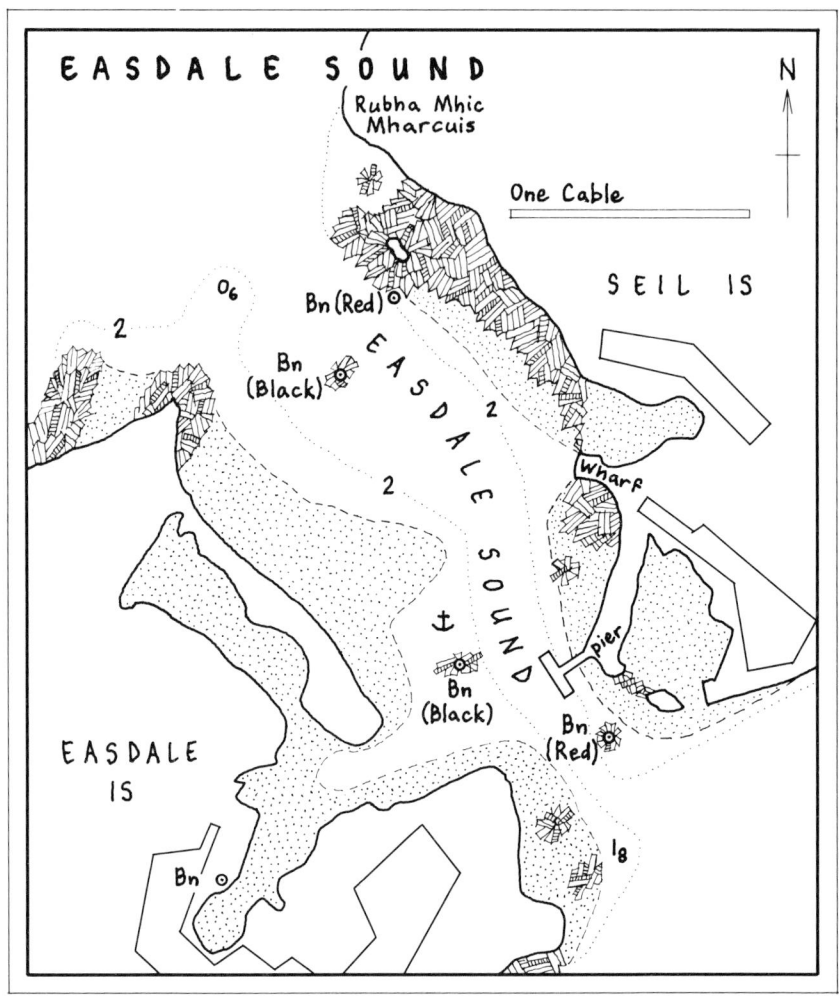

EASDALE SOUND

Rubha Mhic
Mharcuis

N

One Cable

SEIL IS

0_6

Bn (Red)

2

Bn
(Black)

EASDALE SOUND

2

2

Wharf

pier

Bn
(Black)

Bn
(Red)

EASDALE
IS

1_8

Bn

Diesel and water are available alongside a fuelling pontoon, and there is a small chandler. Hull and engine work and winter storage on hard standing (tel. Kilmelford 248 and 279; Ch 16). Shop, hotels etc $\frac{1}{2}$ mile away.

Easdale Sound   (see plan)   56° 17$\frac{1}{2}$'N, 5° 39'W
Approaching from the S, keep well to the NE side leaving the red beacon off the Seil shore close to starboard. The flood runs N: the N entrance can be rough with wind over tide. It may be possible to moor alongside a boat on the wharf, otherwise anchor as shown on the plan: very restricted swinging room. Shops, P.O. and hotel on the Seil side.

Eilean nam Beathach (Puilldobhrain)   (see plan)   56° 19$\frac{1}{2}$'N, 5° 35'W
Tidal range 2·3m at mean springs, 0·9m at mean neaps

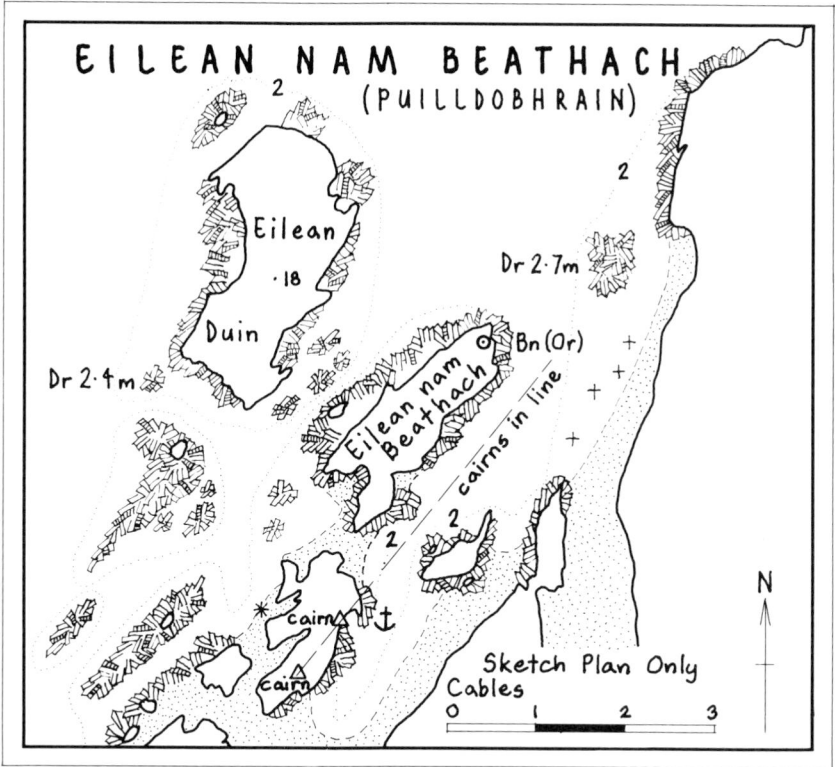

For those using chart 2169, Beathach is the island SE of Eilean Duin. Locally known as Puilldobhrain (pron. 'Pull-doran'), this is an excellent anchorage, although it seems to have acquired a reputation as a great beauty spot for which I can see no real justification. It is pretty, but I would have thought not outstanding by the very high standards of West Scotland.

The only hazard in the approach is an offshore drying patch that covers only at HW springs, NE of Eilean nam Beathach. If the tide is high enough to cover this, it is avoided by keeping well over to the NE point of Beathach, approaching on a course of no more than 190°Mag. The island can be identified by a beacon on its NE end; in 1979 this was orange, but it may have to be repainted when IALA buoyage reaches the area. From here, steer for the NE end of the islet to the S to avoid a rock E of the S end of Beathach, more extensive than the chart shows. Keep 50m off this islet to its S end, and then proceed S and anchor E of the island S of Beathach. Good holding in mud with little weed. Two cairns on this latter island lead clear of the inner rocks, but the line must not be joined until S of the N tip of Beathach.

Loch Feochan   56° 21′N, 5° 32′W
An extremely difficult entrance, and the loch higher up is tricky, so chart 2387 should be carried and it should not be attempted by the inexperienced. The tide runs at about 5 knots in the narrows, the ebb continuing for 2 hr or so beyond the time of local LW.

The entrance to Loch Feochan. Low water, but the ebb is still swirling out.

The entrance channel carries about ½m at LWS, but as the tide does not turn until 2 hr after LW Oban there is about 1·8m in the entrance at LW slack at springs, and fractionally more at neaps. Shallow draft yachts can therefore enter with the first of the flood stream and feel their way in, but others are advised to enter and leave at HW slack.

The channel is right over on the N side as far as Ardentallan Point; after that it divides, and the best water is to be found by proceeding diagonally across to the SE shore and steering parallel to that about 100m off. The anchorage is in Ardentallan Bay about a mile NE of the narrows, opposite the wide but drying mouth of a burn. Good shelter and no great stream.

An alternative anchorage sheltered from all but N winds is Barnacarry Bay, outside the narrows. Anchor in 4m, sand, a cable WSW of the islet in the E part of the bay: at HW the long drying reef that runs NE from Rubha Garbh Airde covers, and at such times it is most important to approach and leave the bay from or to well E of N. Do not go more than 100m S of an E–W line through the islet, as the S part of the bay is very shallow. No facilities or stores.

Loch Spelve   56° 23′N, 5° 42′W
This loch on Mull, on the W coast of the Firth of Lorne, offers a useful bolt-hole in bad weather from the W.

The approach channel keeps close along the N side of the entrance as far as the point where the cliffs end and the shore turns from a northwesterly to a westerly line. About 300m beyond this corner there is a drying patch about 150m offshore, and one must steer to pass this spot nearly but not quite as far S as midstream; there is also a wide shoal patch coming out from the S shore. Chart 2171 shows this quite clearly before it blanks out. Fortunately there are no hidden hazards further into the loch. The tide runs in and out at about 3½ knots at springs.

In bad weather the W bay of the N arm of the loch is less subject to squalls. Anchor in the SW corner of the bay in 7m, mud and shell. More beautiful, though, is the anchorage about 350m short of the extreme end of the SW arm of the loch, 12m, mud. This is little more than a mile from the towering peak of Ben Creach, over 2000ft high, and there are beautiful walks in the area, for instance along the N side of Loch Uisg to the W and on to Lochbuie about 3 miles to the WSW. No supplies.

Little Horseshoe Bay   (see plan of Kerrera Sound)   56° 23′N, 5° 32′W
The anchorage is inside a drying shoal, marked by a red buoy to its S. Pass

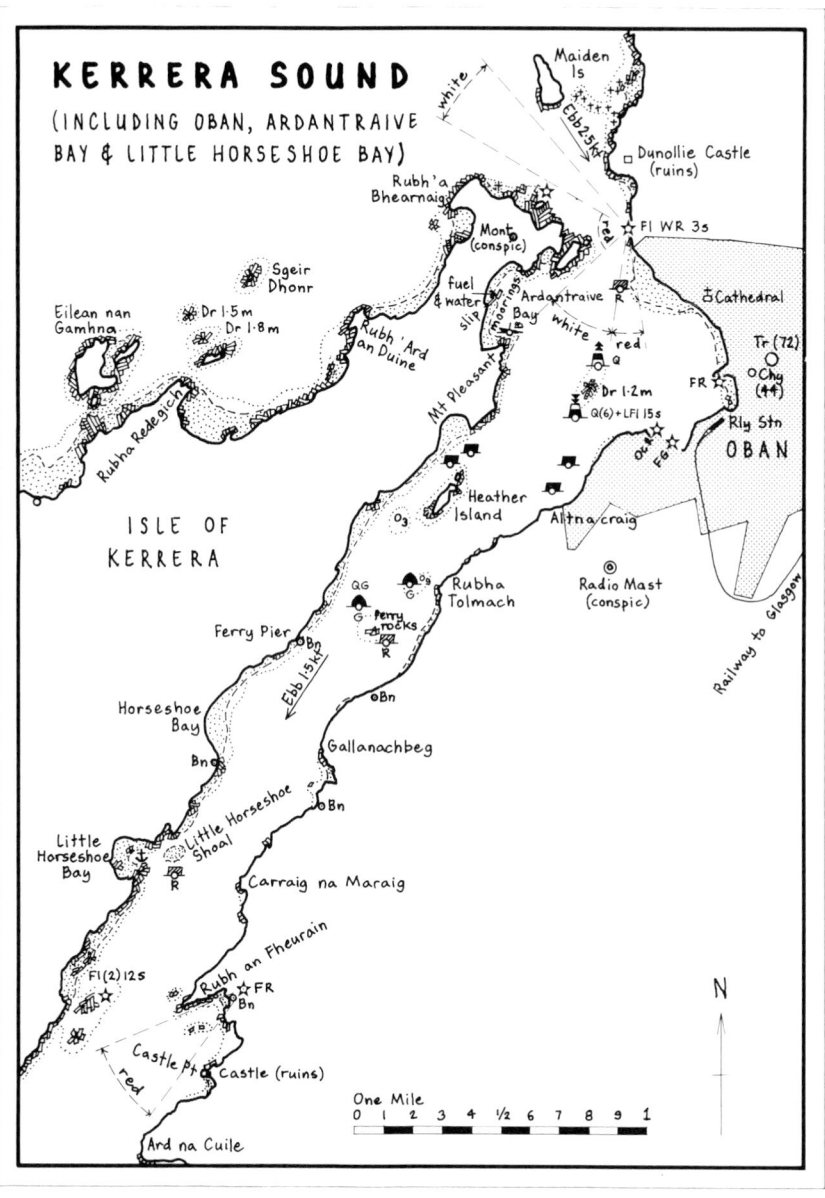

Ardentraive Bay and Hutcheson's Monument

close S of the buoy and steer NW into the bay, giving its S arm a wide berth. Anchor in 5m, mud; there are some moorings and the bottom is foul in places. No supplies.

Ardentraive Bay, Oban   (see plan of Kerrera Sound)   56° 25′N, 5° 30′W
Tidal range 3·3m at mean springs, 1·1m at mean neaps
This is really the yacht harbour for Oban, as Oban itself is very exposed to W or NW winds and has no satisfactory anchorage, while its wharves are completely exposed.

The S arm of the bay extends into a long reef, with a drying wreck near its N tip. If the wreck is visible it is safe to round it about 50m off: on the rare occasions when it covers, keep going N up the sound until the end of the jetty bears 290°Mag. before turning into the bay.

Once in the bay a mooring is needed, as there is really no room left to anchor in reasonable depth. Either pick up a buoy or go alongside the fuelling pontoon and enquire at the office of Oban Yacht Services Ltd (tel (0631) 63666). Be prepared for occasional steep rolls while on the moorings, as passing steamers send considerable wash into the bay. Fuel and water alongside the pontoon at the end of the jetty; repairs, chandlery, slipping etc. It is the best part of a mile row over to Oban, but it is often possible to get a lift in the company's launch.

It is perfectly possible to tie up alongside at Oban in calm or easterly weather, but a nasty sea can get up very quickly if it begins to blow even moderately from the W, and boats should on no account be left unattended. The best berth is usually on the wharves NW of the railway station. Oban is the main town in this part of Scotland: there are shops, hotels, banks, and trains and buses to Glasgow.

Passage notes: Oban Bay to Fort William and the Caledonian Canal
Before completing the passage notes to Ardnamurchan Point, this important
branch must be dealt with: not only is it a beautiful cruising area in its own
right, but it also leads to the Caledonian Canal and thus by a sheltered route
to the North Sea. Charts 2378, 2379 and 2380 will be needed if this area is to
be included in the cruise.

The N end of Kerrera Sound presents no problems, as long as allowance is
made for the ebb stream which attains 2½ knots at springs. From here the
direct route is by the Lynn of Lorne. Note the reef off Rubha Garbh-Aird,
and a lesser one off Rubha Fion-aird: pass E of Eilean Dubh, close either side
of Branra Rock (beacon), and close W of the buoy W of Appin Rocks
(beware tidal streams setting across these). The best exit is then midway
between Inn Island and Sgeir Bhuidhe, marked by a lighthouse, Fl (2)
WR.

If passing between Shuna Island and the shore, a course keeping the W side
of Appin House (the higher of two conspicuous houses, see photo) in line
with Knap Point, carries 1·7m at MLWS. From here there are no hidden
hazards more than ½ mile offshore until the spit running S from the E side
of the Corran Narrows. Most of this carries 1·8m at MLWS, so it is seldom a
real problem for yachts; it is buoyed at its end, and the less extensive shallows
at the other side are also buoyed. The flood can exceed 5 knots through
Corran Narrows, the main force being from 4 hr before to HW Oban; the
main force of the ebb is 2–5 hr after HW Oban, with a maximum rate of nearly
4 knots. From here to Fort William the only hazard is a spit off the mouth of

Knap Point in line with the left end of Appin House (the higher building) carries
1·7m at MLWS.

Dunstaffnage Bay. If taking the ground be sure to be E of the sewer pipe.

Connel Bridge, Loch Etive, glowing in a flash of sun. Pass under where shown, but at your own risk.

the River Kiachnish, but at Fort William the loch is narrowed by wide sand-banks on the E side and later rocks and shoals on the W side, and it is vital to keep within the well buoyed channel. Tidal streams are unimportant for the whole passage except in the Corran Narrows and the entrances of some of the side lochs.

Dunstaffnage Bay   56° 27′N, 5° 26′W

A most useful anchorage, being the other yacht harbour within reach of Oban and having the advantage that it is within walking distance at a pinch. The approach is between Rubhagarbh and Eilean Mor and is straightforward. There are numerous permanent moorings but plenty of room to anchor clear of them. The sand in the S part of the bay is clear and smooth, and bilge-keelers may prefer to anchor closer in and take the ground: but beware of the sewage pipe which lies on the surface of the sand (see photo). Land at the pier, or inflatables can be carried up the beach at the S of the bay to near the road. Buses or a 3 mile walk to Oban, where all supplies are available. Marina development is planned.

Loch Etive   56° 27′N, 5° 24′W

Tidal range inside Connel Narrows: 1·8m mean springs, 0·7m mean neaps.

Loch Etive enjoys one of the most frightening entrances I have ever encountered, and it should only be attempted by experienced skippers with reliable power and steady nerves. A shelf across the narrows just E of the bridge (15m clearance) causes the water level to vary visibly between one side and the other, giving the waters the name Falls of Lora. Heavy turbulence is found W of the Falls, especially on the ebb. The passage should only be attempted an hour either side of slack water, which occurs about 2 hr after LW and HW Oban. Enter at the LW slack, when the drying patches are visible, and aim to pass under the bridge just to the left (N) of the bottom of the main strut running diagonally down and left from the right-hand apex of the bridge (see photo). Once through, steer NE to avoid an uncharted spit off the point N of Connel, and keep 100m off the N bank through the next narrows as the whole of the S side is shoal. There are strong eddies and ripples NE of these narrows, but they are harmless.

The loch is very short of good anchorages: the best I found was in the SE corner of Linne na Craige in 6m, stiffish mud: CQR best. Avoid the bay W of Airds Point, which looks perfect but has a squishy mud bottom which gives no holding. The upper part of the loch is not covered by Admiralty Charts: I have explored it using the Ordnance Survey map but do not recommend this practice! The wind tends to funnel up the loch and blow onshore into all the bays: altogether I must advise against a visit except in settled good weather and by a boat with a strong and experienced crew.

Loch Creran   56° 32′N, 5° 25′W

Tidal range 3·3m at mean springs, 1·2m at mean neaps

The entrance to this loch is foul on the Eriska side, so Glas Eilean and the Dearg Sgeir light should be left fairly close to port. Once the turn to the southward opens up, however, steer over to leave Rubha nam Faoileann

Creggan Bridge, Loch Creran. The power line is invisible, but the supports can be seen on both sides.

fairly close to starboard to avoid the rocks off Woodhall. The flood runs at 4 knots through the narrows at springs. The traditional anchorage is off South Shian, E of the S end of Eriska, but I prefer the bay E of Rubha Riabhach, good holding in sand, 5m; no facilities. To visit the head of the loch a second set of narrows have to be negotiated, under a bridge with 12m clearance. There is also an electricity cable, marginally higher than the bridge but to seaward of it, so do not attempt this passage unless your masthead is less than 12m above the waterline!

To pass under the bridge keep to the S arch, but well over towards the centre pier. Approaching, keep the S-facing wall of the centre pier open, but only just: this clears the rocks in the centre arch, and also the spit that runs out from the S shore at the W end of the narrows. On the best line there is about 2½m at half-tide. Beyond the bridge, keep to mid-channel until the loch widens, then slightly to the S side to avoid the long spit running out from the N shore. There is good anchorage in the SE corner of the inner loch in 8m, mud. No supplies.

Dallens Bay   56° 35′N, 5° 23′W
Tidal range 3·4m at mean springs, 1·2m at mean neaps
This pretty anchorage is sheltered from all but N winds. Approaching from the S, the left hand edge of Appin House (the higher of two conspicuous white houses) in line with Knap Point gives a minimum of 1·5m at MLWS. Anchor in the middle of the bay as far S as soundings allow, remembering that most of it dries. Good holding in sand and shingle. Supplies at Portnacroich, ½ mile to the S.

Loch Leven   56° 41′N, 5° 11′W
Tidal range not known
The approach to the loch is straightforward from the S: from the N due
allowance must be made for the Cuil-cheanna spit, though a normal yacht
can cut at least ½ mile N of the buoy which marks its end. Keep well N of
Nos. 1, 2 and 3 mooring buoys, and approach the bridge on a line which
enables you to see right down the loch: this leads clear of the extensive
shoals off Ballachulish. Streams attain well over 5 knots under the bridge at
springs, but there are no hazards as long as the boat is kept in mid-channel.

Poll an Dunain   (see inset on chart 2380)   56° 41½′N, 5° 10′W
The best anchorage for anyone not exploring the whole loch. Note the spit
running out from the shore E of the hotel, and keep 100m from the S shore
until Eilean na-h-Luraiche bears no more than 30° Mag. before turning up into
the bay. If leaving on the ebb, beware of the stream setting you onto this
spit. Pass midway between the beacon marking the rocks W of Eilean na-h-
Luraiche and the islet (which looks like mainland) to its W and anchor as
soundings allow clear of moorings. Sand and weed, moderate holding. No
supplies, Loch Leven Hotel ¼ hour walk.

Kinlochleven   56° 43′N, 4° 59′W
Passage up the loch presents no problems using chart 2380. Keep well to the
N side through the second narrows; the flood stream reaches 6 knots and the
ebb 4¼. The loch is subject to heavy squalls. Anchor off the S shore near the
wharf in 5m, rather steep-to and holding suspect. Stores in the village.

Camas Sallachain (Shallachan Bay)   56° 42′N, 5° 18′W
Tidal range 3·7m at mean springs, 1·6m at mean neaps
Open to the SW, when Camas Aiseig provides an alternative, but a useful

Ballachulish Bridge, Loch Leven

Night falls at last over the anchorage of Poll an Dunain, Ballachulish. Anyone for ski-ing tomorrow?

anchorage to spend a night on the way from or to the Caledonian Canal. Anchor about a cable NE of the three islets in the W part of the bay, 5m, sand and mud. No supplies.

Camas Aiseig   56° 43½'N, 5° 15'W
Open to the NE (when see above) but a good staging point for the canal in southwesterly weather. From the S keep about a cable offshore, sounding carefully, to pass inside the Corran shoal, and anchor off the Ardgour shore in 2–4m, sand and shell. Best anchorage is for the next 400m after passing the hotel pier.

Corpach   56° 50½'N, 5° 07'W
It is possible to anchor off the S end of Fort William in 4–5m, but it is exposed and the holding is doubtful, so this should only be used as a short-term shopping stop, with someone left aboard.

Moorings are laid outside the sea lock, and one may be available: enquire at the Corpach Chandler & Sailing School (tel Corpach (039 77) 245). The owner. John Cuthbertson, can supply diesel in cans, and Calor gas. Users of the canal will prefer to lock in and lie comfortably in the basin between the sea lock and the first of the canal locks. The water level there can fall considerably as a result of locking and leakage, so warps should not be made up too taut if securing near HW. Good range of chandlery, and good shops in the village.

The Caledonian Canal

The canal is about 54 nautical miles long, of which about 35 consist of Lochs Lochy, Oich and Ness. There are 29 locks: 15 between Loch Linnhe and the summit reach which includes Loch Oich, 100 ft above sea level, and 14 down to the Inverness Firth. All the locks are manned. There are also ten swing bridges. The locks can be violent, especially the sea locks if entered near LW, but all can produce a good swirl when going uphill, and strong warps and cleats and good fenders are needed. In 1979 several of the locks were in poor repair. It is unwise to count on getting through in less than two *full* days: in the summer season locking can be much slowed down by numerous charter motor cruisers. The locks operate only from 8–12 and 1–5 (apart from the sea locks, which will open at other times for an extra fee), and the keepers will not start a boat down or up a flight unless she will complete the passage by closing time. It is technically possible to get through in a single day, and it can sometimes be done out of season, but most readers will be using the canal in summer when two full days should certainly be allowed, and even then there will be no time to waste during working hours. Fees are considerable (over £25 for 30ft LOA in 1979), but I was charged no extra for leaving the boat on a jetty in the canal for a week while I nipped home. Dues are payable at the Corpach end, and a splendid chart of the canal reprinted from an ancient Admiralty chart is available for a small fee. Water and diesel are available for shallow draft boats (up to about 4ft) from a jetty about 4 miles from the Inverness end, owned by a cruiser charter firm.

Passage notes: Oban to Ardnamurchan Point

Tides run strongly, up to 4 knots, off the E coast of Mull, and considerable races occur S and W of Lismore Island. These cannot be wholly avoided, but it is usually best to pass between Lismore light (which actually stands on Eilean Musdile, not Lismore itself) and Lady's Rock, but look out for strong cross-sets. Once inside the Sound of Mull streams slow down to a maximum

Duart Castle. To the right of the picture is the entrance to the Sound of Mull.

The anchorage at Craignure Bay. Owing to a change of wind *Kuri Moana* is rather too close inshore, but the holding is good.

of 2 knots in the narrows N of Craignure, and less further up the sound. A yacht on passage will keep NE of Glas Eileanan (lt Fl 6s) and later, just for a change, Eileanan Glas (also Fl 6s, just to avoid any confusion!) and then well over to the Mull side to avoid the rocks off the NW of Morvern opposite Tobermory. From Ardmore Point it is plain sailing to Ardnamurchan.

Craignure Bay   56° 28′N, 5° 42′W
Tidal range 3·4m at mean springs, 1·3m at mean neaps
A useful anchorage, although if the wind comes round to the NE even a gentle breeze kicks up a disgusting chop. This has happened to me, but luckily the holding is very good so the result is extremely uncomfortable but not actually dangerous. Anchor at the SE end of the bay on the line of the stone pier and about 100m off its end in 4–5m, good holding in mud and sand but there is thick kelp.

Land at the stone pier. There is an inn near this landing, and a good shop opposite the root of the ferry jetty, with a phone box between. Water hose on the ferry jetty in the middle of the bay, but it is rough to lie alongside, and only practicable in calm conditions near HW. The Isle of Mull Hotel lies at the NW end of the bay, and I have dined exceptionally well there, with a beautiful view of the sound and Lismore Island; last orders are about 8.15, which is late for this part of the world, but if you are going to be late it is safer to ring (tel Craignure (068 02) 351). It is a fair walk from the stone pier, though, so allow plenty of time: it might well be quicker to row and land just below the hotel, an unmistakeable long, low building, but take boots as the ground is marshy.

Loch Aline   (see plan)   56° 32′N, 5° 46′W
Tidal range (est.): 4m at mean springs, 1½m at mean neaps
The upper reaches of the loch are full of hazards, and chart 2390 is needed.
The entrance is well buoyed and straightforward, however, and the plan
shows it and the only good anchorage, which is at the S end of the loch. The
leading beacons are very hard to spot, the rear one having a black S cone
topmark, and the front being a pinkish perch (1979), but they are quite
unnecessary for yachts, who merely need to leave each successive buoy fairly
close on the appropriate side. The tide sets through the narrows at up to 2½
knots. Anchor as shown on the plan in 5–6m, good holding in mud. Shops,
P.O., hotel at Lochaline W of the narrows.

Fishnish Bay   56° 31′N, 5° 50′W
This bay is clear of dangers, but does dry 2 cables or more from its S shore.
Anchor in the middle of the bay in 5–6m; mud, sand and shingle. Open to N
and NW winds. No facilities.

Salen Bay, Sound of Mull   56° 31′N, 5° 57′W
Tidal range 3·5m at mean springs, 1·4m at mean neaps
From the E this bay must be approached with care, passing close S of the
black (soon green) conical buoy marking Bogha Rock, and then close N
of the pier on Rubha Mor, and so to the red can buoy marking Antelope
Rock. Turn S just short of this (or pass E of it if approaching from the N and
W) and anchor a cable S Mag. of the buoy, W of the root of another ruined
pier, in 4m, gravel and shell. Shops, hotel etc in Salen.

Tobermory   56° 37′N, 6° 03′W
Tidal range 3·7m at mean springs, 1·5m at mean neaps
The narrow channel between Calve Island and the mainland of Mull should
not be attempted without surveying at LW, as the base of a disused beacon
lies just below the surface when there is enough water to go through. The N
entrance is wide and clear. There is little room to anchor near the pier owing
to moorings, and where there is room depths are likely to be at least 15–20m.
There is always plenty of room and good shelter in the Doirlinn a Chaibhe,
the NW part of the channel between Calve Island and Mull, the best place
being about 400m short of the peninsula at the S end of Calve Island in 10m,
though this is about a mile from town.
    Tobermory is an extremely pretty place (to my mind it goes fractionally
'over the top', but I shall probably be assassinated for saying so!), and offers
all possible facilities in the way of shops, hotels etc. Water and diesel at the
E end of the quay.

Loch Sunart
To explore the length of this beautiful loch, which is some 18 miles long,
chart 2394 must be carried, but the westernmost anchorage, in Loch Droma
Buidhe, can be reached using only 2171 and the directions below.
    Crossing from Tobermory to Auliston Point, two rocks, Big and Little
Stirk, lie almost directly in the way. Big Stirk only covers at exceptional
springs, so if Little Stirk is covered the safest route is to pass 1–2 cables N of
Big Stirk. Proceeding up the loch, the narrows N of Risga look alarming but

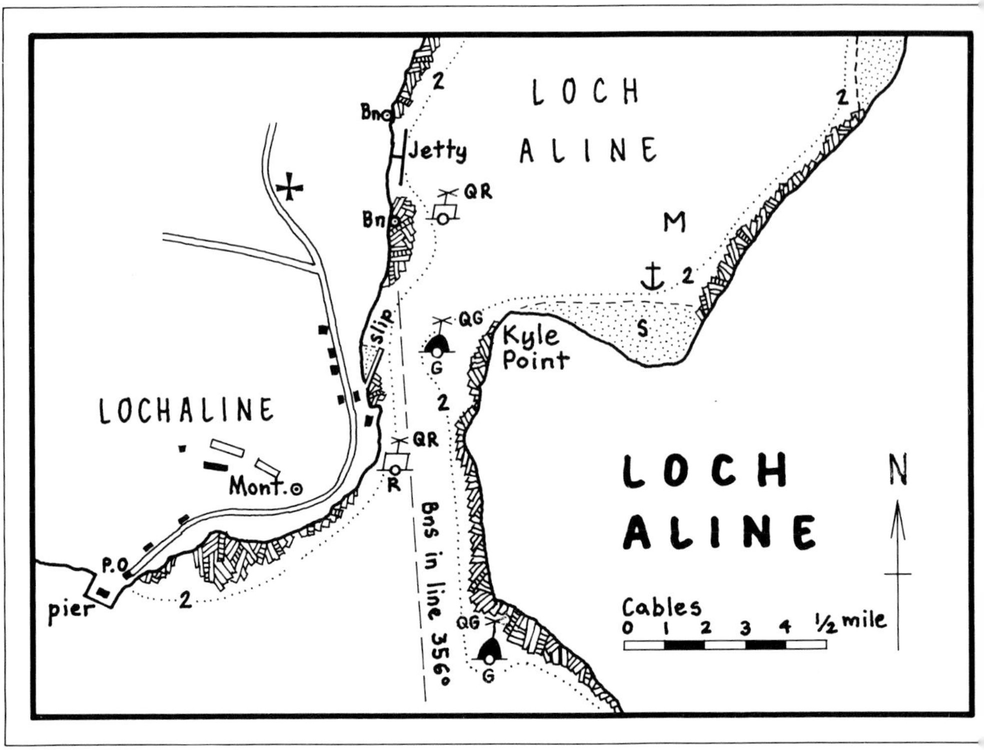

LOCH ALINE

Bn○

Jetty

Bn○

QR

S/P

QG

G

2

QR

R

Mont.⊙

P.O.

pier

2

LOCHALINE

Bns in line 356°

LOCH ALINE

M

⚓ 2

S

Kyle Point

QG

G

LOCH ALINE

N

Cables
0 1 2 3 4 ½ mile

2

2

Loch Aline entrance, Sound of Mull

are in fact much safer than the wide S route, which has Broad Rock right in the middle. Give a good berth to Dun Ghallain, which has a drying rock a cable off; then all is easy until the loch bends round towards the S. Here there is a most tricky area: the intrepid reader who wishes to go further will do best to use the two transits of 339° and 294° shown on the chart until Garbh Eilean bears NE Mag.; then steer for Rubh' an Dunain until soundings fall to 10m; after which course can be altered to Glas Eilean, which is passed close on its S side. From here to the head of the loch is straight forward. Near LW the shoal running WNW from Glas Eilean (1·8m at MLWS) may have to be looked out for. Note that the tides run at $2\frac{1}{2}$ knots in the narrows N of Carna, and up to $3\frac{1}{2}$ knots in the Laudale Narrows.

Loch na Droma Buidhe   56° 39$\frac{1}{2}$′N, 5° 57′W
Tidal range 3·7m at mean springs, 1·5m at mean neaps
This is the loch that lies S of Oronsay, near the entrance to Loch Sunart, a fact which I mention as it is unnamed on chart 2171. The entrance is clean along the narrows, but just where the loch widens right out there is a 1m rock almost dead in the middle. Avoid this by keeping well over to the N

Tobermory, Mull

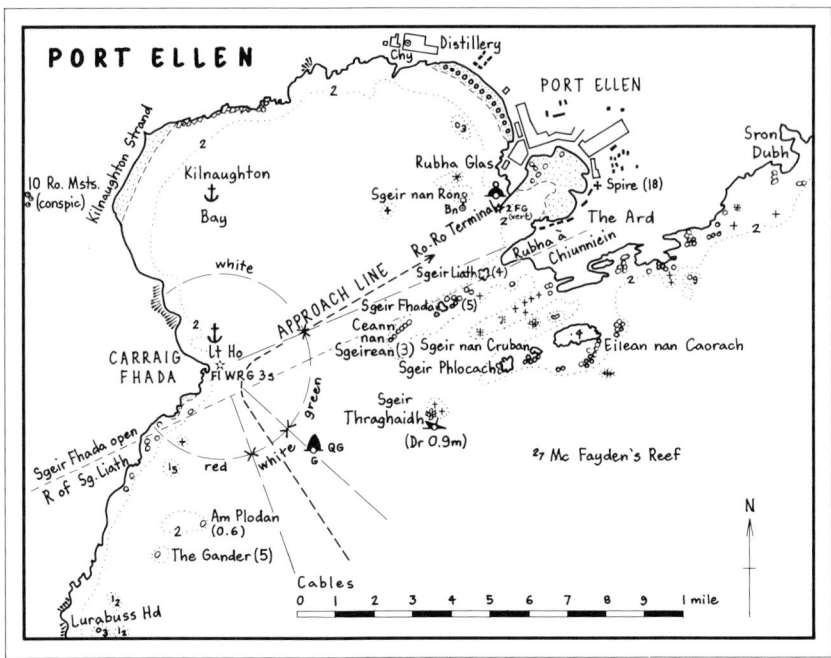

PORT ELLEN

side until the first deep bay (which has a small islet in it); from the mouth of this bay steer approx 210°Mag. for a gap in the cliffs on the S shore. Anchor as soon as soundings drop to 12m, good holding in mud. A beautiful, peaceful and sheltered anchorage; no supplies.

Loch Teacuis   56° 39′N, 5° 53′W

I hesitated to include this loch at all, and I must make it quite clear that the entrance is very difficult, and should only be attempted without sail up and under reliable power, by an experienced skipper.

Enter E of Carna, keeping close along the Morvern (SE) shore until 200m short of the barrier of rock that almost closes off the channel. At this point steer boldly NW and then curve round W and SW, passing close W of the end of the rock barrier. From here keep slightly W of the middle of the visible channel for about 2 cables, when the second barrier is met. This is a headland projecting from the SE shore of Carna; it has a shelf of rock off it, and a large rock, Sgeir Liath, which covers at HWS, 50m to its SE. The rock must be passed on its E side about 10–15m off, after which steer 210°Mag. into the middle of the upper pool of the loch. If Sgeir Liath is covered, the entrance should not be attempted without local advice. When a position is reached from which the head of the loch can be seen, turn SE for the second narrows. The danger here is the rock drying 1·2m in mid-channel: it is avoided by keeping N of mid-channel through this part of the narrows.

Good anchorage in perfect shelter can be had anywhere in the SE half of the inner pool, mud bottom, 3–6m. No stores. Note that the spring rate through the first entrance is 2½ knots, flowing S on the flood and N on the ebb. The ideal time to enter for the first time is at half ebb, when the foul stream gives more time for sounding and identifying rocks, and they will be uncovered: only when the lie of the channel is known is it advisable to enter with a fair tide.

Salen Bay   56° 42½′N, 5° 46½′W
Tidal range 3·5m at mean springs, 1·7m at mean neaps
This is the main place for shopping, repairs etc in Loch Sunart. The drying shoal in the middle of the entrance is marked by a beacon on its *west* side with a N cone (starboard-hand beacon), and another with a red can on its *east* side: vessels trying to pass between these come to a sudden stop with a grinding crunch! Pass E of the more easterly beacon, and anchor anywhere to the N of the shoal as space allows (plenty of room usually, good holding in mud), or pick up a free mooring and check ashore with Conyer Marine (tel Salen (096 785) 654 or try Ch 16 when in sight). The firm can do most repairs, and has a chandlery. There is a hotel at the top of the bay (look for a long conservatory on the front), P.O. 200m N of the pier and shop 200m further on.

Garbh Eilean   56° 41½′N, 5° 41′W
Good anchorage in perfect shelter can be found between this island and Rubha an Daimh, 10m, clay. Keep on the 294° transit until the SE face of the island opens, then steer midway between island and headland and anchor when soundings fall to 10m.

Strontian   56° 41′N, 5° 33′W
As far as I know, this is the only one of our anchorages to have a chemical element named after it! The anchorage is E of the bay, which dries so far out that it is wise to keep well over to the S shore until the monument on the E arm bears N Mag. before crossing to the N side of the loch and anchoring in 4–6m, mud, ESE of the pier. Stores and pub in village, ¾ mile walk.

There is no useful harbour between Tobermory and Ardnamurchan, so the notes on Loch Sunart conclude this section.

3 MULL OF KINTYRE TO ARDNAMURCHAN POINT BY THE OUTER ROUTE

Passage notes: Mull of Kintyre to Port Ellen
This is a quite straightforward passage once the tide-rips off the Mull itself have been cleared. The difficulties come later on, in rounding Islay to the westward.

Port Ellen   (see plan)   55° 37′N, 6° 13′W
Tidal range 0·6m at mean springs, 0·3m at mean neaps
This harbour offers good shelter, but only shallow draft yachts can use it to the full: others have to anchor off.
   Lines of islets and reefs stretch WSW from the Ard, so a good offing should

be maintained until Carraig Fhada light bears at least 320° Mag. before steering for it. (At night, keep in the white sector.) Keep on this line until Sgeir Fhada can be seen clear open to the right of Sgeir Liath, when it is safe to steer for the harbour entrance.

For deep-draft boats, the most comfortable place is often to anchor in the bay N of Carraig Fhada light, or further N in Kilnaughton Bay (3–4m rock, and 6–7m sand and shingle, respectively). Otherwise it is possible to anchor outside the pierheads: a riding light is needed and one may be disturbed by wash. Shallow draft boats can get in and lie alongside the inner part of the pier in 1–1½m: note the very small tidal range. The town is of some size, with good shops, bank, hotels etc. No special yacht facilities. Islay is of course the centre of malt whisky distillation; Laphroaig and its famous distillery are only a mile E of Port Ellen.

Passage notes: Port Ellen to Ardnamurchan Point by the western route
Heavy overfalls are found off the two SW headlands of Islay, the Oa and Rhinns Point, and spring rates reach 6 knots off the Rhinns. It is therefore important to time the tides correctly and avoid wind over tide conditions. The NW-going tide runs from 1 hr after HW Dover to 6 hr before (say HW Greenock to 5 hr after), so going W and N the best time to leave Port Ellen is about HW Dover, when with luck a fair tide can be carried as far as Iona. However, once clear of Islay the timing is not critical, as further N the spring rates only attain 1·2 knots.

Until the shelter of Tiree, 60 miles N of the Oa, is reached, this passage is open to the full Atlantic swell, and the seas can be wild, especially where the bottom has shoaled from 50m to 10m in a mile or two, as happens SW of Colonsay and of the Ross of Mull. Both areas should be avoided in bad weather, and navigation is tricky in poor visibility as there are drying rocks a long way offshore. It would be a rash skipper indeed who tried to make the Sound of Iona from the S in fog: much better to find the relatively clean NW coast of Colonsay and work round the N end and into Scalasaig. Some 6–8 miles W of Iona is another area of underwater mountains, and heavy overfalls and breaking seas can be met here, but once N of this point the remainder of the passage to Ardnamurchan Point is straightforward, and enjoys increasing shelter first from Tiree and then Coll.

Readers intending to use this route, passing through the rocks W of the Ross of Mull and the Sound of Iona, would be well advised to carry chart 2617. In any case they should take careful note of the fact that the Sound is shoal right across from the village to 2 cables off the E shore ¼ mile N of Fionnhport. Best water for those making a through passage (no less than 1·6m at LWS) is found by keeping 100m off the Iona shoreline between the beginning of the village and the cathedral. If stopping at Bull Hole, coming from the S leave the two starboard buoys in the sound close to starboard, then steer just E of the S point of Eilean nam Ban (see notes and plan for Bull Hole, below).

Bowmore   55° 46′N, 6° 17′W
This useful anchorage lies towards the head of Loch Indaal, a deep lagoon leading off the bay between the Oa and the Rhinns of Islay. The entrance is

Port Ellen: a yacht can be seen in the anchorage near the lighthouse.

absolutely straightforward by day or night as long as the shore between Saltpan Point and Bowmore, which is shoal, is given a wide berth. Pass N of the two beacons off Bowmore, and anchor a cable or so N of the NE one in about 3m, good holding in sand. The anchorage is safe but uncomfortable with a southwesterly swell. P.O., shop etc in village.

Nave Island   55° 53½′N, 6° 20′W
Tidal range 3·0m at mean springs, 1·2m at mean neaps
A strategically important anchorage, lying on the N coast of Islay, N of the entrance to the (un-navigable) Loch Gruinart. It is exposed to the NE but protected from the really big swells which come from W or SW on this coast. Approaching, the Balach Rocks which cover at high springs, must be avoided, either by keeping close to the Islay shore from Rubha Bhoisa to Gortantaoid Point or, from the N, getting the E end of Nave Island in line with Ardnave Point while still well out, and approaching on that line until the point of the island can be rounded about 200m off. Anchor with the E end of Nave Island bearing 010°Mag., about halfway between the island and Ardnave Point, 5–6m, sand. If the wind is northerly it is possible to sound carefully along the Islay side until S of the W end of the HW mark of Nave Island, which gives better shelter. No supplies.

Loch Tarbert, Jura   55° 57½′N, 6° 00′W
Tidal range 3·1m at mean springs, 1·3m at mean neaps
Chart 2481 must be carried if this loch is to be fully explored, but the outer anchorages can be used with only chart 2169. They are Bagh Gleann Righ Mor, exposed to the SW, and Glenbatrick Bay, exposed to the NW. To enter the inner loch pass close S of the southernmost Gleann Righ islet and then Aird Reamhar. Then steer to pass close S of Sgeirean an Rubha Liath until the white beacon marks behind Rubha nan Meann on the S shore come in

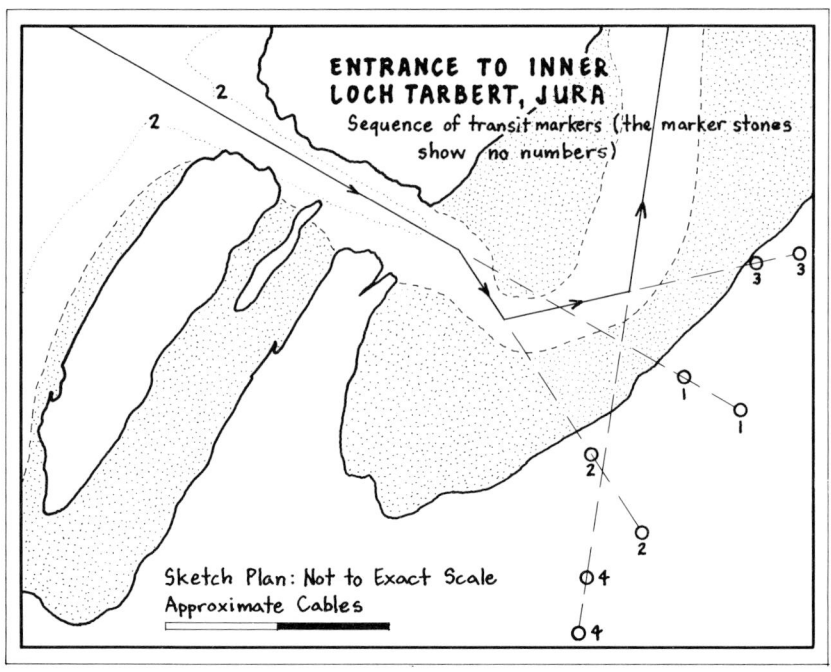

ENTRANCE TO INNER LOCH TARBERT, JURA
Sequence of transit markers (the marker stones show no numbers)

Sketch Plan: Not to Exact Scale
Approximate Cables

line. This line can be held until 200m offshore, when the S bank is held closely between Rubha nan Meann and Rubh' a Choire, keeping halfway between the 4m high rock pinnacle and the S shore, which leads through the first narrows.

The innermost loch is not charted by the Admiralty, but it can be navigated by those who like that sort of thing on a series of beacon transits, each one being held until the next two beacons come into line. It is reached through Cumhann Beag, and there is 5ft at *low* water neaps (say 2ft at LWS) on the best line. The only problem is immediately on emerging from Cumhann Beag (55° 58′N, 5° 53′W), when one is confronted by a bewildering array of white stone leading marks all visible at once. The sketch plan shows how the first ones are to be followed: once on the way up the loch each pair comes in sight when embarked on the previous transit, so there are no problems as long as a sharp eye is kept out: always turn onto the *first* transit to come in line if two are visible at once. This is a fascinating cruise, and I recommend it to all who share my love of sailing in apparently impossible places!

Bagh Gleann Righ Mor   55° 58′N, 5° 58½′W
The more westerly of the two anchor symbols shown on the N shore of Loch Tarbert on chart 2169 is in this bay. Anchor 1 cable S of the point at the W side of the bay, 6m, mud. Some swell in SW winds, and subject to squalls in northerlies. No supplies.

Glenbatrick Bay   55° 57′N, 5° 59′W
The anchorage is just E of the N end of Rubhachan Eoghainn (the point

The inner narrows, Loch Tarbert, Jura

½ mile E of Rubh' a Chois-aoinidh). Approach the point on about 160° Mag. (two beacons will be seen in line) and then turn E round the point when no more than 100m off, to avoid the drying rock 200m off the point. Anchor E of the N end of the point in 2–2½m. Open to the NW. No supplies.

Eilean Ard   55° 58′N, 5° 54½′W
A perfect anchorage once through the first narrows: anchor N (1·5m) or NE (2m) of the northern tip of Eilean Ard, softish clay, perfect shelter, highly recommended. Supplies? You must be joking! Not a house in sight. It is also possible to anchor pretty well anywhere in the inmost loch, though the holding may be rather soft.

Oronsay   56° 01′N, 6° 13′W
Tidal range 3·4m at mean springs, 1·1m at mean neaps
Good anchorage can be found just north of the Admiralty anchor marked on chart 2169 in the bay SW of Eilean Treadhrach, on the E side of Oronsay. Sound carefully and keep over to the E bay, behind the shoals that project SW from the point of Eil Treadhrach. Subject to scend in strong easterlies. No supplies.

Scalasaig Harbour, Colonsay   (see plan)   56° 04′N, 6° 11′W
Tidal range 3·4m at mean springs, 1·1m at mean neaps
There is room for four or five yachts to anchor in the harbour in about 3–5m, S of the pier, but care must be taken not to obstruct the steamer, which comes alongside the pier on its windward side. Otherwise anchor in Loch Staosnaig

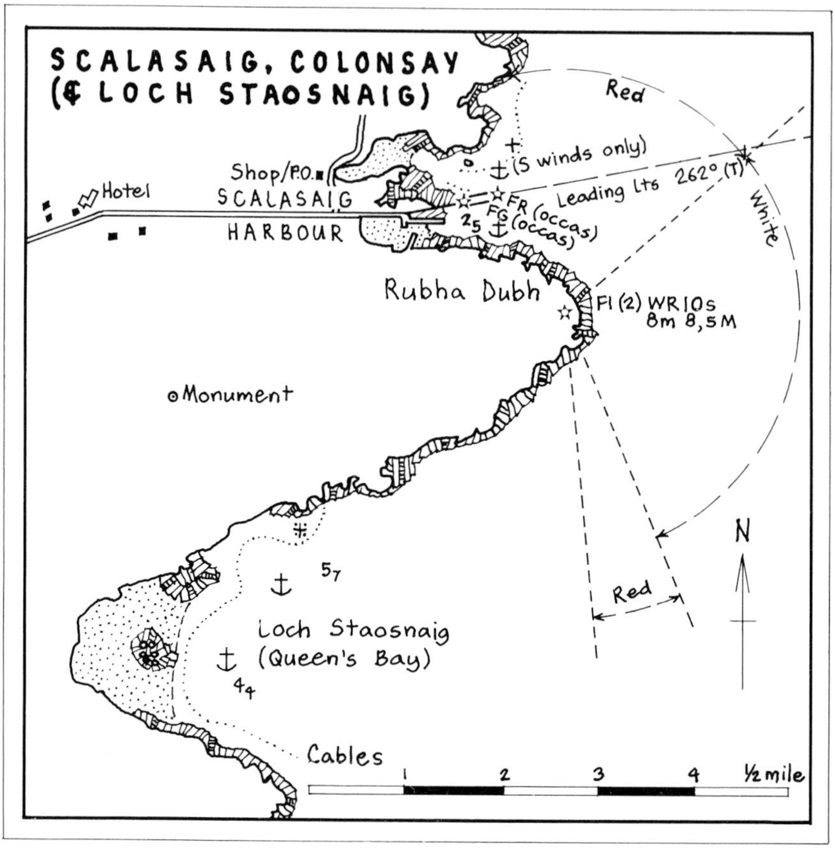

SCALASAIG, COLONSAY
(& LOCH STAOSNAIG)

Red

Shop/P.O. ■

Hotel

↧ (S winds only)

SCALASAIG

☆ FR (occas)

Leading Lts 262° (T)

White

HARBOUR

FG (occas)

2₅ ↧ (occas)

Rubha Dubh

☆ Fl (2) WR 10s
8m 8,5M

○ Monument

N

↥

Red

↧ 5₇

↧

Loch Staosnaig
(Queen's Bay)

4₄

Cables

| 1 | 2 | 3 | 4 | ½ mile |

The anchorage at Rubh' Ardalanish

(locally known as Queen's Bay), good holding in 4m, sand, near the head of the bay. Beware a drying rock patch 100m off the N shore of the bay about half way in. Both harbour and bay are wide open to the E, when Oronsay is to be preferred although it is uncomfortable.

A hotel in the village provides bar snacks, baths and dinners by arrangement; the owner can arrange petrol and diesel in cans, and supply water. Good shop/P.O.

Carsaig Bay, Mull   56°19′N, 5°59′W
Tidal range 3·5m at mean springs, 1·3m at mean neaps
An anchorage on the S coast of Mull, 2 miles W of the entrance of Loch Buie. It is protected by offshore islands and shoals, but would still not be advisable in strong winds with S in them. The entrance is straightforward except near HW, when the shoals cover: in such conditions enter from the E, allowing for shoals extending E from the most easterly island farther than the chart suggests. Keep no more than a cable from the line of the N shore of the islets, and anchor N of the gap between the two main islands in 4–5m, good holding in sand with patches of weed. At the W end there is an uncharted extension of drying shoal running out on a bearing of about 300°Mag. from the most westerly islet, which improves the shelter of the anchorage but makes the W entrance inadvisable at half-tide for strangers.

Rubh' Ardalanish   (see plan)   56° 16′N, 6° 16′W
Tidal range 3·5m at mean springs, 1·4m at mean neaps
A popular and certainly very beautiful anchorage on the W side of Rubh'

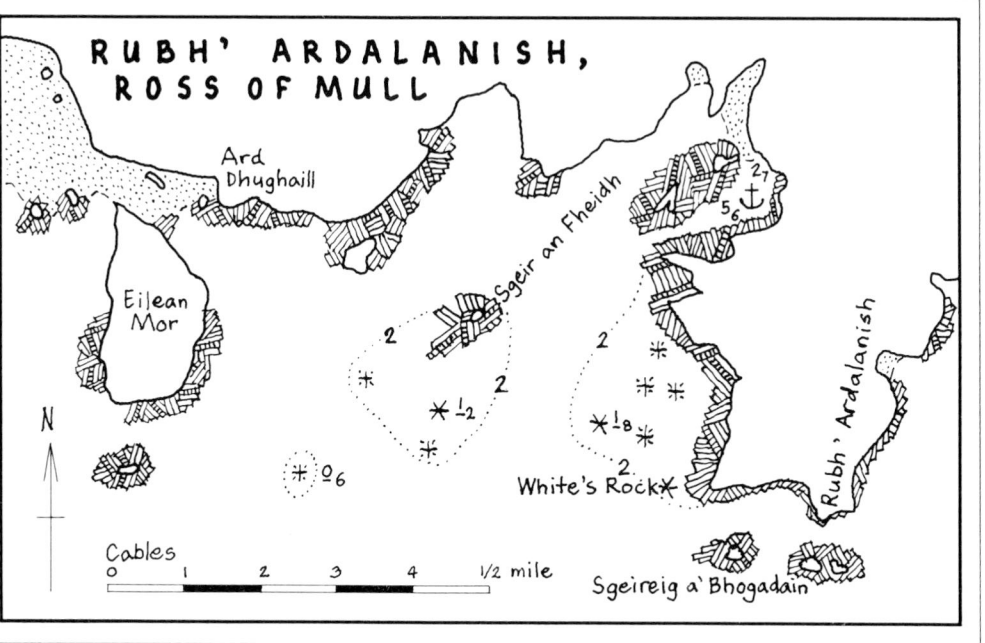

Ardalanish, near the W end of the Ross of Mull. At LW the entrance is easy; near HW identify Sgeir an Fheidh, which never covers, and approach its E side steering N Mag. until the S side of Eilean Mor to the W is in line with the S point of the mainland beyond. At this point turn and steer about 30°Mag. to approach the rocks on the E side of the bay, which are here steep-to. After a blind bay which is obviously exposed, a narrow creek with rocky sides will open up to starboard: the anchorage is in a small lagoon at the head of this creek, 4m, sand and some weed. (The weed line is usually clearly visible, and it is better to drop on the clean sand.) Excellent holding, but far less sheltered than its land-locked appearance would suggest: quite heavy scend gets in in strong winds from between S and W. No supplies, landing difficult.

Eilean Dubh, Ross of Mull   (see plan)   56° 17′N, 6° 21′W
Tidal range 3·5m at mean springs, 1·5m mean neaps
This anchorage is exposed to the SE, but offers perfect peace in conditions when Ardalanish is highly uncomfortable. From a position 1 cable N of Sgeir na Caillich, steer to pass close S of Eilean Dubh. When the island curves away to the N do not follow round, but keep steering 100°Mag. until opposite the middle of the channel between Eilean Dubh and the mainland. At this point, turn N Mag. and anchor as far in as soundings allow. Good holding in clean sand, and a nice beach. No supplies.

Bull Hole, Sound of Iona   (see plan)   56° 20′N, 6° 22′W
Tidal range 3·5m at mean springs, 1·5m at mean neaps
There are no wholly satisfactory anchorages at Iona, but Bull Hole is the best.

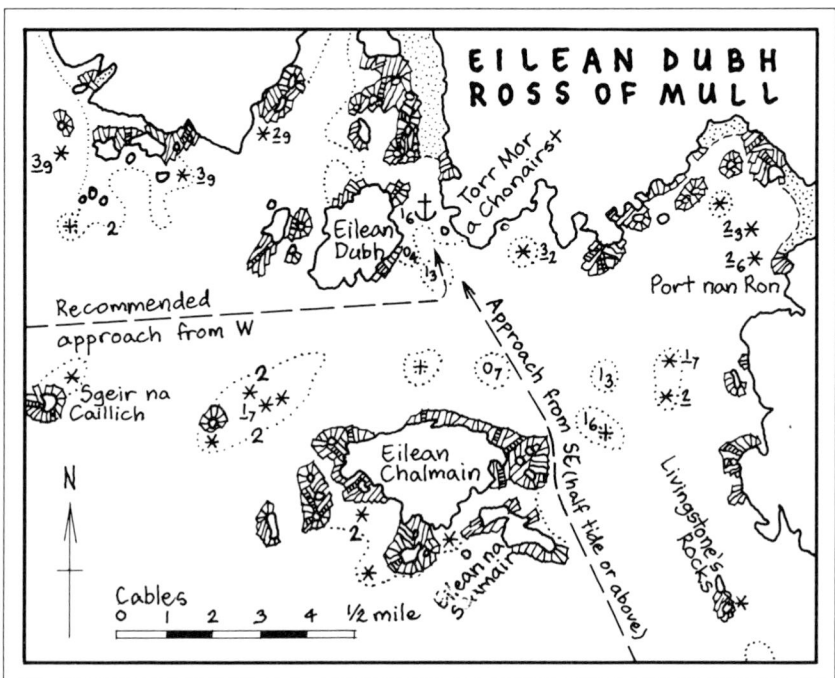

Approaching from the S leave the more northerly starboard buoy *close* to starboard, and then steer for the gap between Eilean nam Ban and the mainland. Do not go an inch W of this line, as it runs close to the E side of the shoal that lies in the middle of the sound. From the N, keep in mid-channel until abreast of Eilean Liath, then steer to pass close to the S of its S end, and from there pass close round the S end of Eilean nam Ban and into Bull Hole.

Anchor in mid-channel clear of the numerous fishermen's buoys: it is safe to go nearly to the N end of Eilean nam Ban, but keep rather to the E of mid-channel to avoid the rock shown. Make sure the anchor is holding well as the tides run fiercely.

In good weather, particularly for a short day visit, it is possible to anchor in Port nam Mairtir (Martyr's Bay) about a cable S of the ferry pier on the Iona side. Sound in as far as draft allows, as the tide runs strongly except close inshore. Good holding in sand, but exposed to swell and wash. However, it is far easier to visit Iona from here than Bull Hole: from there, walk down to Fionnhport and take the ferry, as the tides in the second run too strongly to make the dinghy trip across practicable. The tidal streams given on the charts are seriously understated: as mentioned in a rather inconspicuous note on chart 2617 (but not on 2169 – surely a dangerous omission?), rates in the Sound of Iona attain about $2\frac{1}{2}$ knots. Stores and water, but no alcohol, available in Iona village: there are also (temperance) hotels.

Loch na Lathaich   56° 19′N, 6° 15′W

Tidal range 3·7m at mean springs, 1·2m at mean neaps

There is excellent anchorage in this loch in the SE corner, S of Eilean Ban,

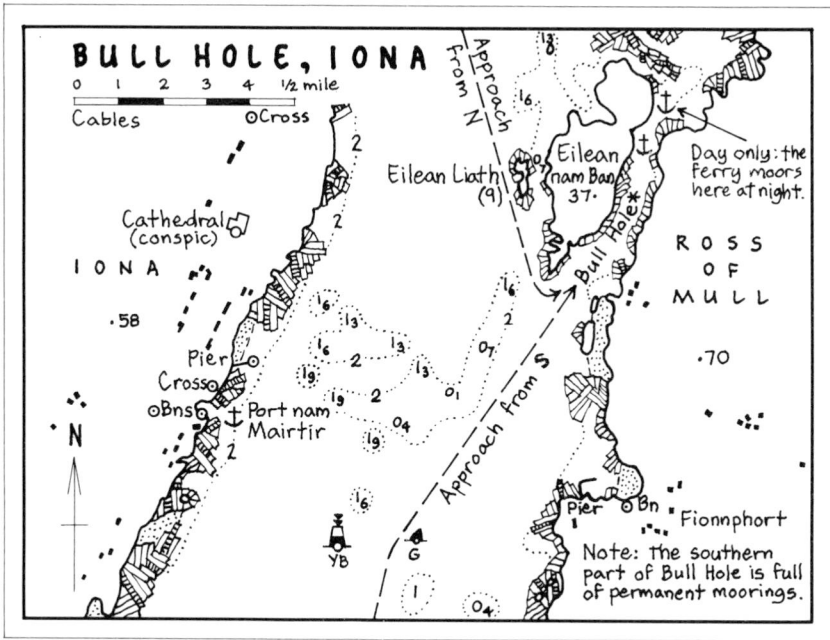

Ben More from Loch Scridain with a force 6 up the loch

the large island near the S end of the loch that is clearly shown though not named on chart 2171. The anchorage is protected from all winds, although in northerlies it is necessary to go in as far as possible behind the island. Stores, water, pleasant hotel at Bunessan, at the SE corner of the loch. The boatyard at Bendoran, a mile away, has moorings and a slipway, hard standing for wintering boats, water and fuel, Calor gas, chandlery and showers. Engine and hull repairs (wood, GRP, steel), Travellift, and a slipway for up to 40T displacement. Tel. (06817) 435 and VHF call sign 'Bendoran'. Fresh fish and shellfish are available from the village or fishing boats.

Loch Scridain (Loch Beg)   56° 23′N, 6° 00′W
Most of this small loch at the head of Loch Scridain dries, so it is necessary to sound carefully when in, but shelter can be found even with a gale blowing straight up the loch by getting as far S as possible once through the narrows. Otherwise the loch is perfectly sheltered. A rather bleak and lonely place: no supplies.

Ulva Sound   56° 29′N, 6° 09′W
Tidal range 3·8m at mean springs, 1·4m at mean neaps
The main danger on the approach to this excellent anchorage is the isolated (and unmarked) MacQuarries Rock. The northernmost islet of the Geasgill Islands in line with the S end of Garbh Eilean (a sheer cliff with a pinnacle

below it) leads safely S of this rock. Keep on the line until Ard na Caillich is clearly visible bearing W of N Mag., and then enter the outer sound. The first mid-channel rock, shown on chart 2171, is marked by a beacon. The rock extends 10m or more N of the beacon, so give it a berth of about 20m (not too much more, as there is another reef opposite) and anchor in mid-channel, good holding in sand, abreast of a second rock which only covers at HWS and 1½ cables SE of the ferry. This is a tricky entrance and the approach should be made with care and while sounding, but I have spent a night there in wild conditions in perfect peace and comfort.

An alternative anchorage in the vicinity is E of Inch Kenneth, about a cable W of the anchor on chart 2171, in 4–5m, mud. No supplies, good shelter except in northerlies. The approach is easy except at HWS, as at other times Maol an Domhnaich is visible, and a line a cable to the E of it and the islets to the S leads into the anchorage.

Bail'a Chlaidh, Gometra   56° 29′N, 6° 16′W
If the covering rock off the entrance, Sgeir na Skeineadh, is visible the approach is straightforward: if not it is avoided by keeping not more than 200m from Rubha Bhrisdeadh-ramh, having approached it from S or W, and running along its E shore at that range. Keep well W of centre through the narrows as the E side is foul. Anchor in about 3m, mud, well short of the cliffy islet at the NW end of the loch. No supplies.

The anchorage in Ulva Sound

Lunga, Treshnish Islands. On the leading line defined by two beacons (arrowed).

Staffa   56° 26′N, 6° 20′W

This island must only be approached in exceptionally calm settled weather, when it is possible to anchor about 150m E of the S tip of the island in about 5m, rock. Be sure to keep S of the landing place (iron railing and steps) and approach from the SE, as all the rest of the coast is foul. An anchor watch should be left aboard in case of dragging or a wind shift. Land at the landing place or in Clamshell Cave just to the N: or there may be a pontoon moored below the refuge hut a cable further N. The island is most beautiful and Fingal's Cave and the others are remarkable, but this is a dangerous place, and a visit should only be attempted, as I have said, in unusually calm conditions, so the reader may have to cruise the area for several seasons before he is lucky enough to get the timing right.

Lunga, Treshnish Isles   56° 30′N, 6° 25′W

A wild and fascinating place NE of the N point of Lunga, perfectly sheltered and yet with a feeling of being in the open sea. The approach from the S is difficult and dangerous, and should only be attempted, if at all, by very experienced yachtsmen with reliable power and under ideal conditions. Chart 2652 is gravely inaccurate on this approach, and 2171 gives a better idea of the line: it is necessary to feel one's way along the W side of the offshore shoals, as they appear and disappear in the never-ending swell. My crew did not enjoy that particular trip!

However, the approach from the N is relatively easy. Tighchoie, which virtually never covers, must be identified N of Sgeir a' Chaisteil and a position made $\frac{1}{4}$ mile NNE Mag. of the N end of this shoal. From here two stone beacons will be seen on Lunga, one on the summit about $\frac{1}{3}$ of the island's width from its right-hand (W) edge, and the other down near the shoreline.

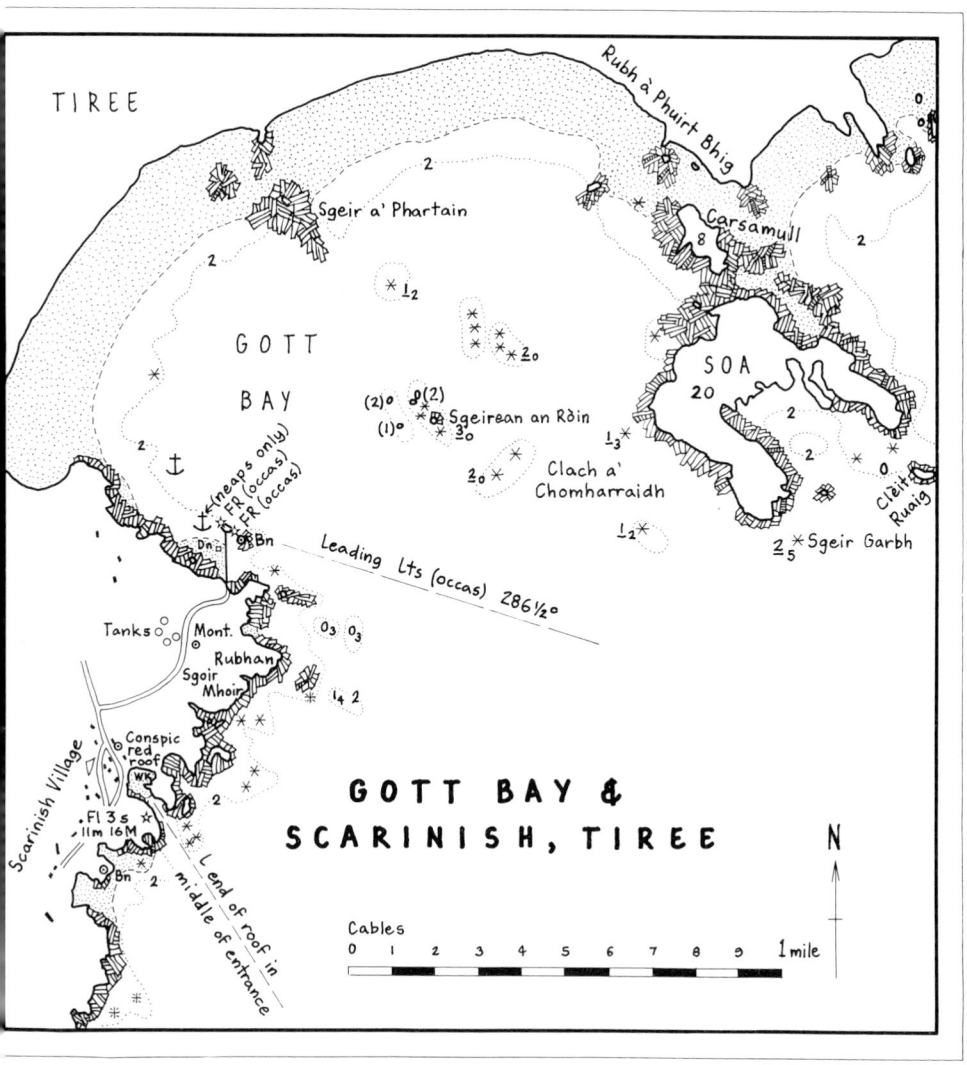

TIREE

Rubh a' Phuirt Bhig

Sgeir a' Phartain

Carsamull

GOTT

BAY

SOA
20

Sgeirean an Ròin

Clach a' Chomharraidh

Sgeir Garbh

Cleit Ruaig

Leading Lts (occas) 286½°

(neaps only) FR (occas) FR (occas)

Dn Bn

Tanks Mont.

Rubhan Sgoir Mhoir

Conspic red roof WK

Scarinish Village

Fl 3 s 11m 16M

Bn

Lend of roof in middle of entrance

**G O T T   B A Y &
S C A R I N I S H ,   T I R E E**

N

Cables
0   1   2   3   4   5   6   7   8   9   1 mile

Keep these in line until level with the N end of Sgeir a'Chaisteil, when it is necessary to ease about 100m E of the line to avoid a group of rocks that just touch the transit. Anchor 200–300m NE of the N point of Lunga, 4m, sand. Good holding and a beautiful place, inhabited only by birds and seals.

Gott Bay, Tiree   (see plan)   56° 31′N, 6° 48′W
Tidal range 3·5m at mean springs, 1·3m at mean neaps
This is the most westerly port in this book, and indeed we are now some 10 sea miles to the W of the Scilly Isles. The island is untypical of the Inner Hebrides, being almost flat, no doubt one of the reasons for its selection as a weather station.

Gott Bay anchorage, Tiree

Scarinish, Tiree. The left-hand end of the long red roof kept midway between the pierheads leads in.

The N part of the bay is full of drying rocks and a long reef projects from the shore SE of the pierhead, but if the S end of Soa is given a berth of about $\frac{1}{2}$ mile a course can then be set for the pierhead until within $\frac{1}{4}$ mile of it, when the heading should be altered to pass a cable or so N of the pierhead. Anchor anywhere beyond the line of the pier as soundings allow: at neaps most yachts can lie inside the line of the T-piece at the end of the pier, 50m or so N of the dolphin, but at springs it is necessary for most keelboats to anchor about 200m NW Mag. from the W pierhead light. The whole area offers good holding in clean sand. Supplies at Scarinish, ¾ mile (see below).

Scarinish, Tiree   (see plan)   56° 30′N, 6° 48′W
Tidal data as Gott Bay
This harbour is perfectly usable by yachts equipped to take the ground, which is all smooth sand, or there may be room to dry alongside the roughish stone pier. Approach on about 340°Mag. and keep the left-hand end of the red roof visible behind the harbour in the centre of the entrance (see photo). There is about 2m alongside the pier at HWN, and 3m at HWS. It is possible to get well into shelter at all states of the tide, as long as the wind is not between E and S when the harbour should not be used. Most readers will find Gott Bay a better bet for spending a night, but Scarinish is a useful place to spend an hour or two near HW if heavy shopping is needed. Shops are good (even a butcher, a rare treat in these parts) and there is a bank. The hotel does bar snacks and meals, baths by arrangement.

Loch Eatharna, Coll   (see plan)   56° 37′N, 6° 31′W
Tidal range: 4·0m at mean springs, 1·7m at mean neaps
This is a particularly beautiful anchorage, and when I have visited it it has been full of rather somnolent seals, who have often escorted my dinghy at a discreet distance, perhaps to see whether my oar strokes disturbed something that would do for breakfast.

The main anchorage is 2 cables or so N of the pierhead. The E side of Eilean Ornsay is clean apart from a 1·8m rock which deep-draft boats must look out for near LW. From here pass about 50m E of Sgeir Charrach, and then steer to pass close outside the pierhead and anchor beyond. Coming from the SE, pass S and W of the Bogha Mor buoy, and then steer for the pier as before. This anchorage is deep (about 7½m); the bottom is rock with heavy weed.

Quieter and better holding is the anchorage E of the N tip of Eilean Eatharna. Approach from midway between Eilean Dubh and Meall Eatharna, and keep in mid-channel until the church tower comes in line with the left-hand edge of the HW mark of the islet N of Eilean Eatharna (the HW line can be seen at low tide as the edge of the weed growth). When these are in line, steer in on this transit and anchor as soundings allow (3–1½m). Sand, with patches of kelp. This anchorage is a little more exposed to SE winds, but quieter in strong winds from any other quarter.

Coll has two good shops and a helpful hotel, which does meals and will arrange baths or showers. Diesel and petrol can be had in cans, and water from the hotel or the café (nearer).

Loch a'Chumhainn, Mull   (see plan)   56° 37′N, 6° 14′W
Tidal range: 3·7m at mean springs, 1·6m at mean neaps
A difficult anchorage that is exposed to the NW, but it is useful in other winds and a convenient place from which to round Ardnamurchan Point, 8 miles to the N.

The entrance should only be attempted by strangers when Sgeir Mhor,

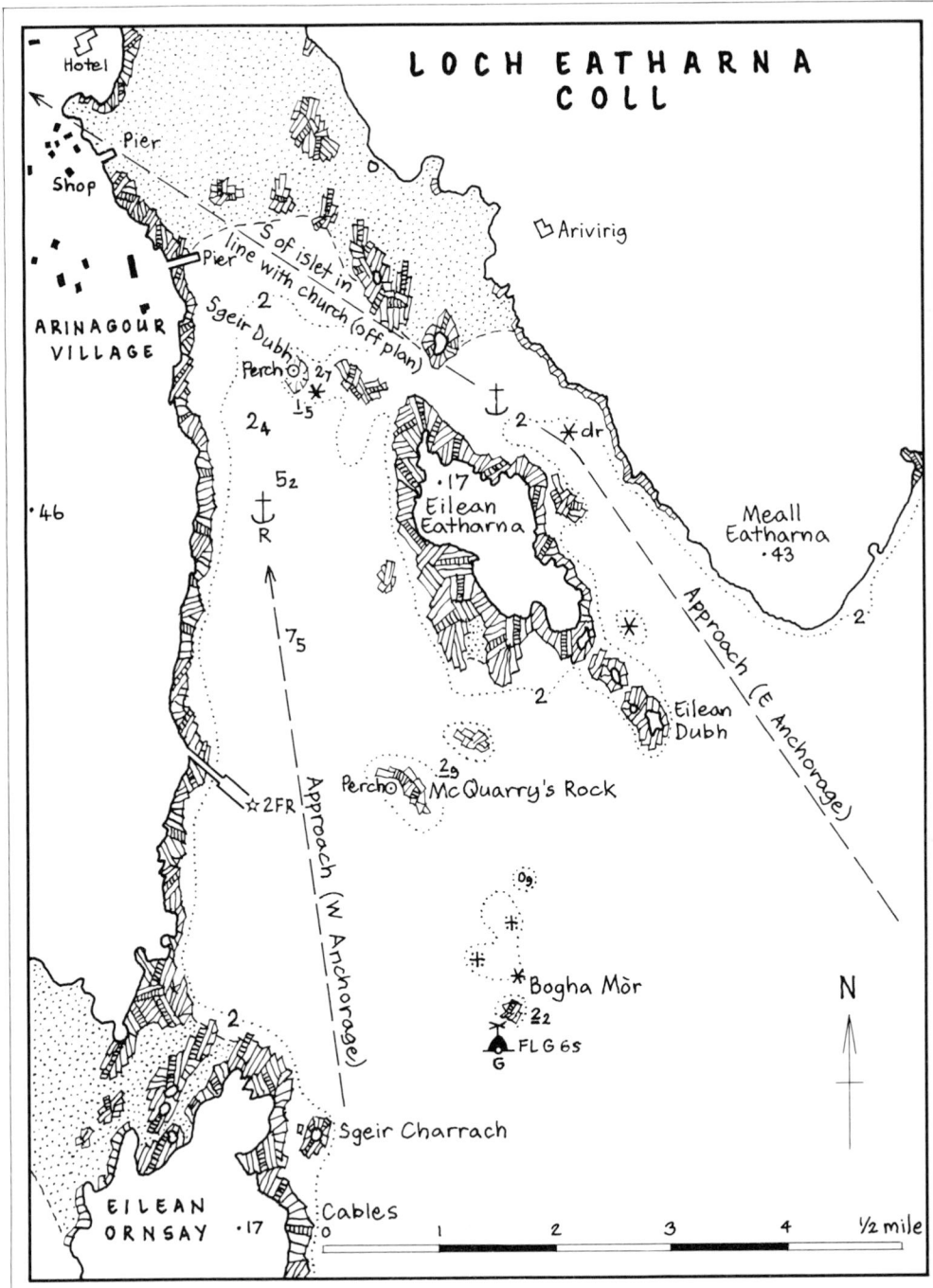

LOCH EATHARNA
COLL

Hotel

Pier

Shop

ARINAGOUR
VILLAGE

Sgeir Dubh

Perch ⊙ 2⁷

1⁵ ⚓ 2

·46

5₂
⚓
R

7₅

☆ 2FR

S of islet in
line with church (off plan)

2

2₄

⚓ 2

✳ dr

·17
Eilean
Eatharna

Eilean
Dubh

2

Arivirig

Meall
Eatharna
·43

2

Approach (E Anchorage)

Approach (W Anchorage)

Perch

2⁹
McQuarry's Rock

0₉

✳

✳ Bogha Mòr

2₂
FL G 6s
G

N
↑

Sgeir Charrach

EILEAN
ORNSAY   ·17

2

Cables
0   1   2   3   4   ½ mile

which is exactly awash at half-tide, is visible. This is not as bad as it sounds, as there is usually enough swell to mark its position even with a metre or more of water over the shoal. Pass 2 cables to the E of it, and then steer S Mag. into the loch. Sgeir Dhearg is usually visible except at very high tide: if it can be seen it can be left a cable to port, and the course held for about another 2 cables to the anchorage.

Anchor in about 3m, sand and shell with some weed, as shown on the plan. No supplies. It would be unwise to use this anchorage to shelter from a

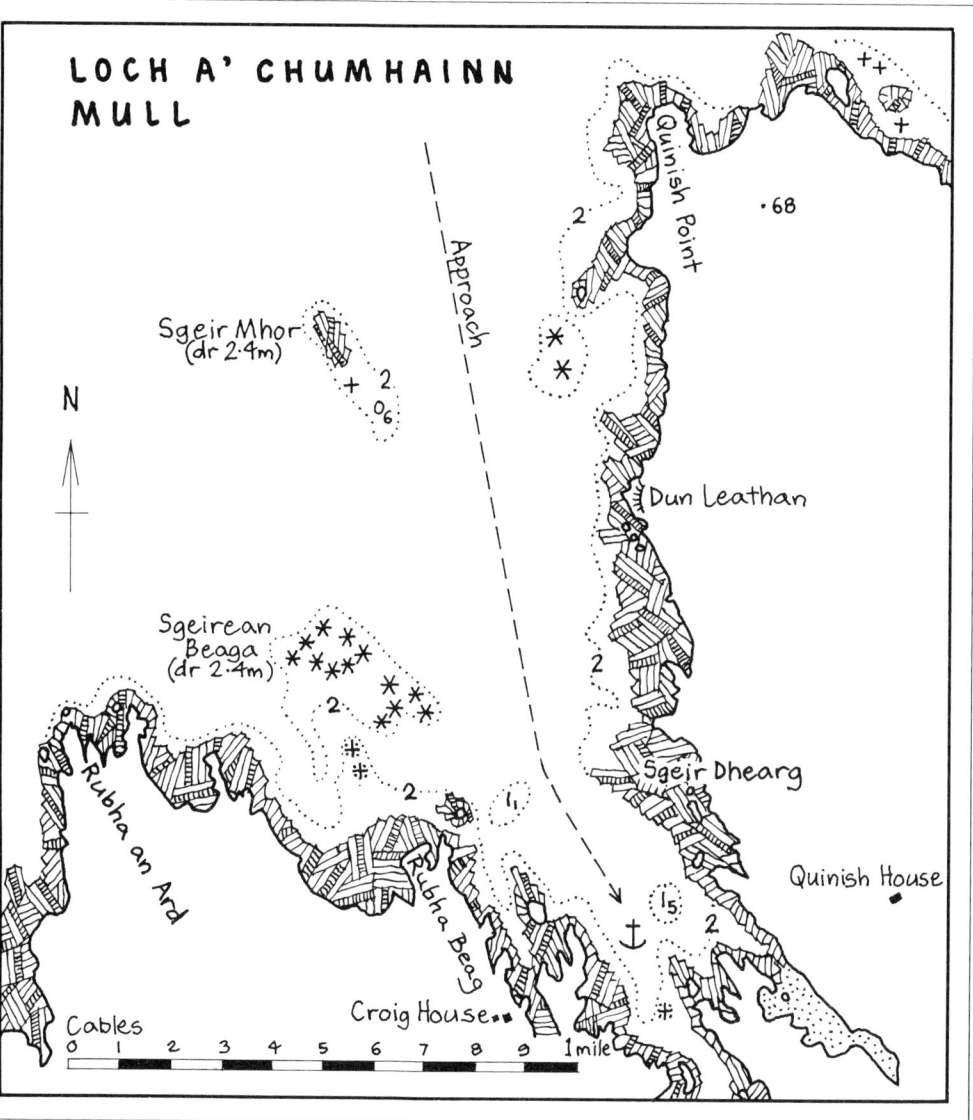

southwesterly gale, as one would be badly placed if it veered to the NW. Running up in such conditions (from Tiree, as it might be) it would be wiser to carry on for 9 miles, mostly in some shelter, to the reliable protection of Tobermory.

Loch a'Chumhainn, being the last anchorage on the outside passage before Ardnamurchan Point, concludes this second section of the book.

III · Ardnamurchan Point to Ullapool

Charts 2207, 2208, 2209, 2210, 1794, 1795 (2541, 2540, 2528, 2534, 2533, 3146, 2509, 2500, 2501)

1 ARDNAMURCHAN POINT TO MALLAIG

Passage notes

As I mentioned in the introductory section, rounding Ardnamurchan Point can be a problem in strong southwesterly, westerly or northwesterly winds, when heavy seas are found in the area. Further north, however, the passage once more runs into a degree of shelter from the Small Isles (Muck, Eigg, Rhum and Canna). There are dangerous rocks up to 2 miles off the north shore of the Ardnamurchan peninsula, so it is safer to keep over to the islands when going north in doubtful visibility. Overfalls which can be bad in heavy weather near springs occur near the Oberon Bank, midway between Eigg and Arisaig, but otherwise there are no offshore dangers to worry about on this passage. North of Mallaig we once more have a choice between an inshore and an offshore route, and these will be dealt with in subsequent sections.

Port Mor, Muck   56° 50′N, 6° 13′W

The nearest harbour (apart from Sanna Bay, useful for fine-weather picnics but no place to spend a night) to Ardnamurchan Point, lying as it does exactly 6 miles to the N. The entrance is narrow and difficult, however: between Dubh Sgeir, an islet that never covers, and Bogha Ruadh, a drying shoal some 150m to its E. The channel is only 50m wide, but it is 10m deep, and is most easily found near LW. The entrance should only be attempted in calm weather, and when Bogha Ruadh can be identified: in any but ideal conditions Eigg is much to be preferred. Once through the narrows, steer for the near end of the cliff on the W side of the bay and anchor in 3–4m. Swell in S to SE winds.

South Channel, Loch Moidart   56° 47′N, 5° 50′W

Tidal range 4·3m at mean springs, 1·9m at mean neaps

This, the first mainland harbour N of Ardnamurchan, is a tricky entrance, although the loch provides perfect shelter once inside. Strangers should not attempt the entrance in fresh onshore winds.

From close W of Farquhar's Point steer to pass close W of Eilean Raonuill. From the NW corner of this island an islet will be seen just to port (N) of the line to the castle near the head of the loch. Steer for the port (W) side of this

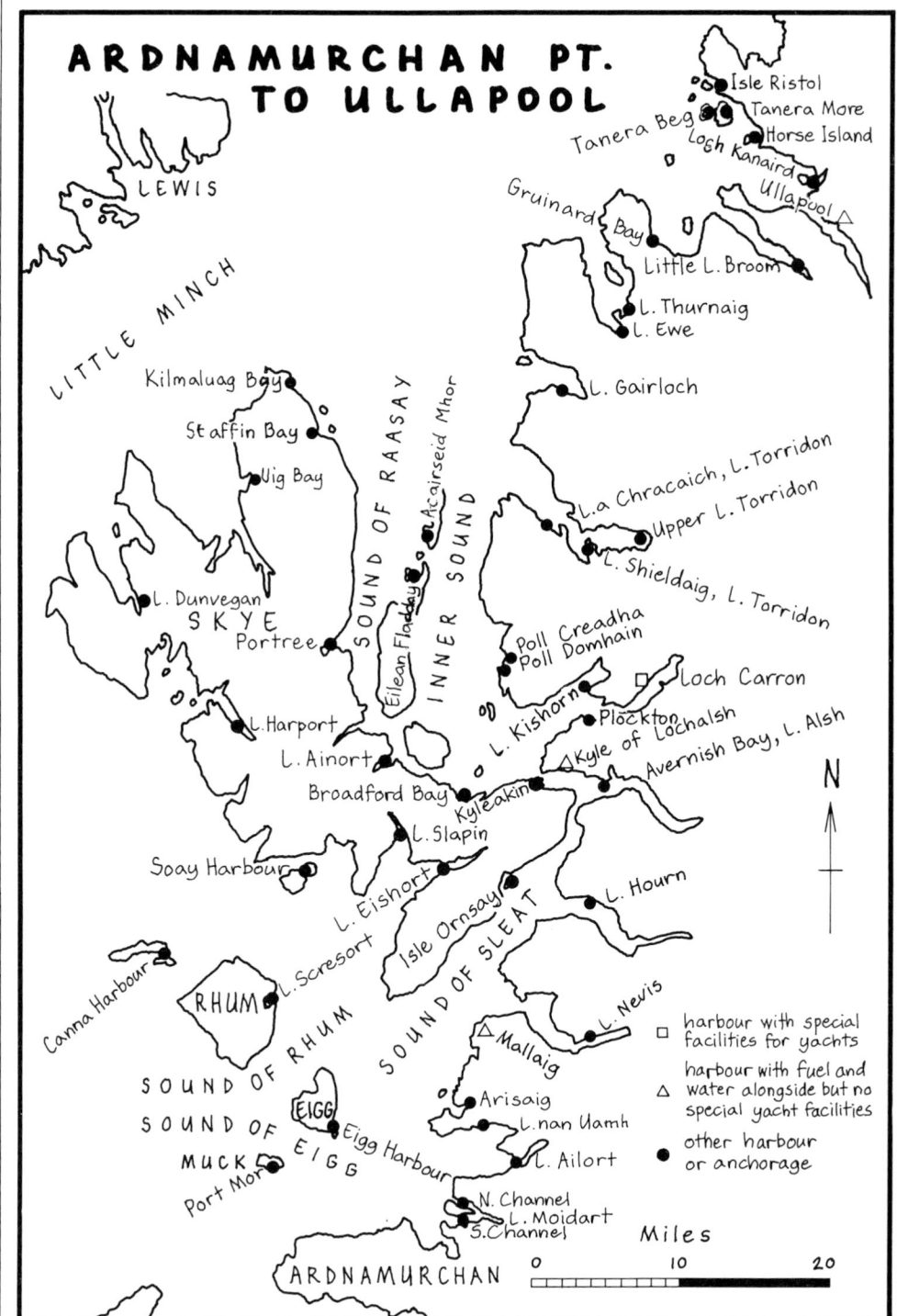

ARDNAMURCHAN PT. TO ULLAPOOL

Isle Ristol
Tanera More
Tanera Beg
Horse Island
Loch Kanaird
Ullapool

LEWIS

Gruinard Bay

Little L. Broom

L. Thurnaig
L. Ewe

LITTLE MINCH

Kilmaluag Bay

L. Gairloch

SOUND OF RAASAY

Staffin Bay

Acairseid Mhor

Uig Bay

L.a Chracaich, L.Torridon

Upper L. Torridon

INNER SOUND

L. Shieldaig, L. Torridon

L. Dunvegan

SKYE

Eilean Flodday

Portree

Poll Creadha
Poll Domhain

Loch Carron

L.Harport

L. Kishorn

Plockton
Kyle of Lochalsh

L. Ainort

Avernish Bay, L. Alsh

Broadford Bay

Kyleakin

N

L. Slapin

Soay Harbour

L. Hourn

L. Eishort

Isle Ornsay

SOUND OF SLEAT

L. Scresort

L. Nevis

□ harbour with special facilities for yachts

Canna Harbour

RHUM

Mallaig

△ harbour with fuel and water alongside but no special yacht facilities

SOUND OF RHUM

Arisaig

● other harbour or anchorage

SOUND OF EIGG

EIGG

L.nan Uamh

L. Ailort

MUCK

Eigg Harbour

Port Mor

N. Channel
L. Moidart
S.Channel

Miles

0   10   20

ARDNAMURCHAN

islet, then turn to starboard and steer to pass close N of a heather topped pyramid-shaped islet (see photo). Beyond this, about 3½ cables to the SE, lies what is a small rock at HW, but becomes at LW a considerable islet with an outlier (see second photo, taken at LWS). This must be left to port, i.e. passed on its S side, giving it a berth of at least 25m. Then steer rather to the W of the SE corner of Shona, and then E along the shore and round to anchor off the jetty in 3–4m, sand. The chart shows the lie of the inner shoals quite clearly, but sound all the way in and have a lookout in the bow: this is a difficult and complex entrance. If going ashore (and it is a most beautiful island) visitors should first go to the big house and ask the owner, Mr Vane, for permission to look round. No supplies.

Entrance to South Channel, Loch Moidart. Taken at LWS: the N end of Raonuill is in the right foreground.

Continuation of entry, South Channel into Loch Moidart.

North Channel, Loch Moidart   56° 48′N, 5° 51′W
Tidal range 4·3m at mean springs, 1·9m at mean neaps
One of the most beautiful anchorages I have ever been lucky enough to visit,
especially when the rhododendrons are in flower in late June, and the entrance
is easier than that of the South Channel, though still tricky and not to be
attempted in strong onshore winds.

From the S, pass midway between the headland on the NW point of Shona
and Sgeir dhu an Iar (remembering that the S two-thirds of the W coast of
Shona is foul up to ½ mile off), and turn SE into the channel. From the N,
identify the islet 300m N of Sgeir dhu an Iar and pass close S of it, keeping
well N of dhu an Iar which has rocks and choal water to its N side. Keep about
100m off the S shore, and when the channel turns NE keep well over to the E
side, as there are rocks well E of the islets in the N part of the channel. There
is at least 4m at half-tide (2m at LWS, and this part of the channel is sheltered
from any swell) all the way in if the best water is found: the ebb stream can
run at over 3 knots.

Anchor near the top of the bay in about 2m; the holding is soft mud and a
CQR is best. If going ashore, ask permission at the big house (Mr Vane) as
for the South Channel. No supplies. Note that this channel does *not* connect
with the South Channel except for a dinghy at HWS.

Loch Ailort   56° 51′N, 5° 47′W
The channel through to the inner part of this loch is too difficult and dangerous to be recommended, but there is a most useful anchorage near the
mouth of the loch, NE of Eilean a'Chaolais. This island has a fascinating
blowhole apparently on its south shore (see photo), and actually on a
detached islet just to its S. There is a dangerous spit running E of this islet:

Blowhole near the entrance to Loch Ailort

The anchorage, South Channel, Loch Moidart

The anchorage in the North Channel, Loch Moidart. Perhaps one of the most
beautiful in Scotland.

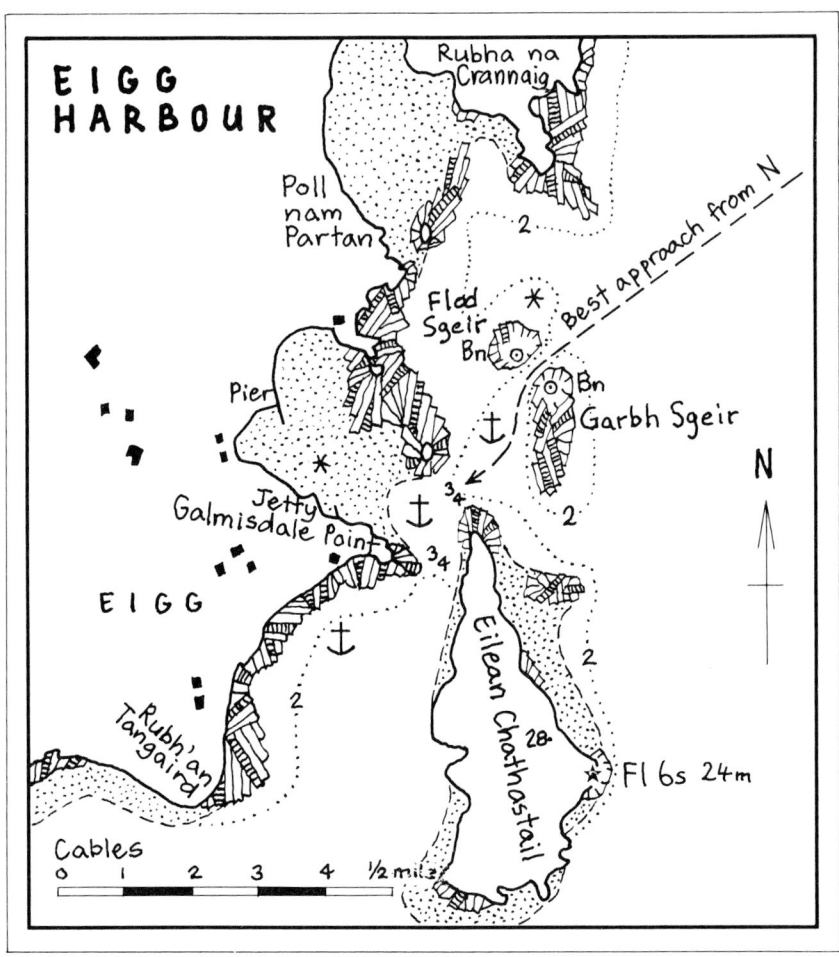

the end of the spit is on the transit between the W shore of Eilean nan Gobhar and the E side of Sgeir Ghlas, so continue E until Ghlas is half hidden behind Gobhar, and then turn N until E of the middle of Chaolais; then approach and anchor in 3–4m, sand. No supplies.

Eigg Harbour   (see plan)   56° 53′N, 6° 08′W
Tidal range 4·2m at mean springs, 1·9m at mean neaps
One of the best harbours in the area, and offers considerable facilities. It can be entered from S or N, and indeed there are two separate anchorages connected by a narrow sound.

From the S, keep well W of the S point of Eilean Chathastail (Castle Island) and anchor on the Eigg side, 6–8m, sand and weed; or proceed through the sound, keeping over to the Castle Island side through the narrows and then steering NW into the main harbour. From the N, one can either pass between the beacons on the N end of Garbh Sgeir (only barely covered at MHWS) and the SE point of Flod Sgeir (dries 3·5m), or approach the N point of Castle Island from just S of E, and curve round it about 100m from the visible shoreline and into the harbour.

The bulk of the harbour dries, but there is room for several yachts to anchor NE of the outer part of Galmisdale Point clear of the permanent moorings, good holding in sand. This anchorage is most uncomfortable in NE winds, when better shelter is to be found in South Bay.

There is a cafe and craft shop near the jetty; diesel from tank there. Shop and P.O. 2 miles' walk – take the more northerly road. The harbour has VHF: call on Ch 16 (working Ch 8): callsign Eigg Harbour. *Eilean Ban Mora*, the 'flagship' of the Eigg fleet, may answer. There are beautiful walks on the island, and in clear weather there is a magnificent view from the summit of the Sgurr.

Loch nan Uamh   56° 53′N, 5° 48½′W

There is an excellent anchorage in the small land-locked bay immediately W of Borrodale Bay. Entering the loch, give An Glas Eilean a good berth to avoid the rocks to its S and E, and steer NE past Eilean nan Cabar and on into Borrodale Bay. Only when Rubh' Aird Mhor bears W Mag. is it safe to turn to port and steer to pass close S of it and curve northward into the little bay beyond. Keep well over to the Aird Mhor side, to avoid the steep and

Eigg Harbour. *Kuri Moana* is lying to *Eilean Ban Mora*'s mooring: the bay soon becomes shoal nearer the Eigg (far) side, but there is plenty of water to anchor nearer Castle Island (foreground).

Loch nan Uamh anchorage. Anchor below the house with the big gable.

dangerous Rafter's Reef off the N of Cabar. Anchor in the mouth of the bay below the conspicuous house (see photo) in 2–3m.

Arisaig Harbour   (see plan)   56° 54′N, 5° 52′W
Approaching from S or N this entrance is easily identified, but it is tricky to pick out when coming from Eigg, largely because Luinga Mhor, so obvious on the chart, is low and flat and often difficult to see. For this reason a white paint mark is maintained on Rubh' Arisaig: if this is approached on a course of between 100° and 120°Mag. it is safe to continue to within a cable of the shore, from where continue along the N shore of Rubh' Arisaig until the first red (actually fluorescent orange in 1979) buoy shown on the plan is seen. The perch marked on chart 2207 near the entrance was missing in 1979, but the rock on which it stood covers only at HW springs. Once this rock has been left to port the rest of the channel is well marked by perches and buoys. If approaching from the S, take care to give the W end of the Arisaig Promontory a berth of at least ½ mile in bad weather: the outer dangers never cover, but at high springs they are nearly awash.

Anchor off the village clear of the moorings, or one may be available from Arisaig Marine (tel Arisaig 224). Water and diesel from alongside the pier, which dries at LW but has 2m or so at half-tide. Shops, hotel, repair facilities. Trains to Glasgow.

Loch Scresort, Rhum   57° 01′N, 6° 16′W
This dramatic anchorage on the E side of Rhum is wide open to easterly winds, but otherwise offers good shelter, though subject to squalls under some conditions. Keep rather towards the N shore when entering, and anchor in sand, 3–4m, near the head of the loch. Stores and P.O. in the village at the head of the loch.

Canna Harbour 57° 03′N, 6° 29½′W

Lying between the islands of Canna and Sanday, this harbour offers good shelter except in easterlies, when some swell gets in, although this is more uncomfortable than dangerous. Approach Rubha Carrinnis from the NE, then continue SW, and turn NW along the Sanday shore to avoid the drying patch W of the pier on the Canna side. Do not go too far in as most of the area dries; anchor as soundings allow in 3–4m. If easterlies are in prospect, the further N towards Canna church the better the shelter. No supplies.

Mallaig (see plan p 109) 57° 01′N, 5° 49′W

Tidal range 4·3m at mean springs, 1·7m at mean neaps

This is an excellent harbour, in my experience providing good shelter even in northerly winds, to which it appears to be exposed. It is a busy fishing port and some of the fishermen are not well disposed towards yachts – nor indeed towards each other sometimes, as there are Scottish west coast and east coast crews there, who do not always agree. Keep well clear of commercial traffic and try to enter or move inside the port in daylight.

A major new extension on the Steamer Pier goes out approx. ENE for 120m, giving much better protection to the harbour but of course requiring

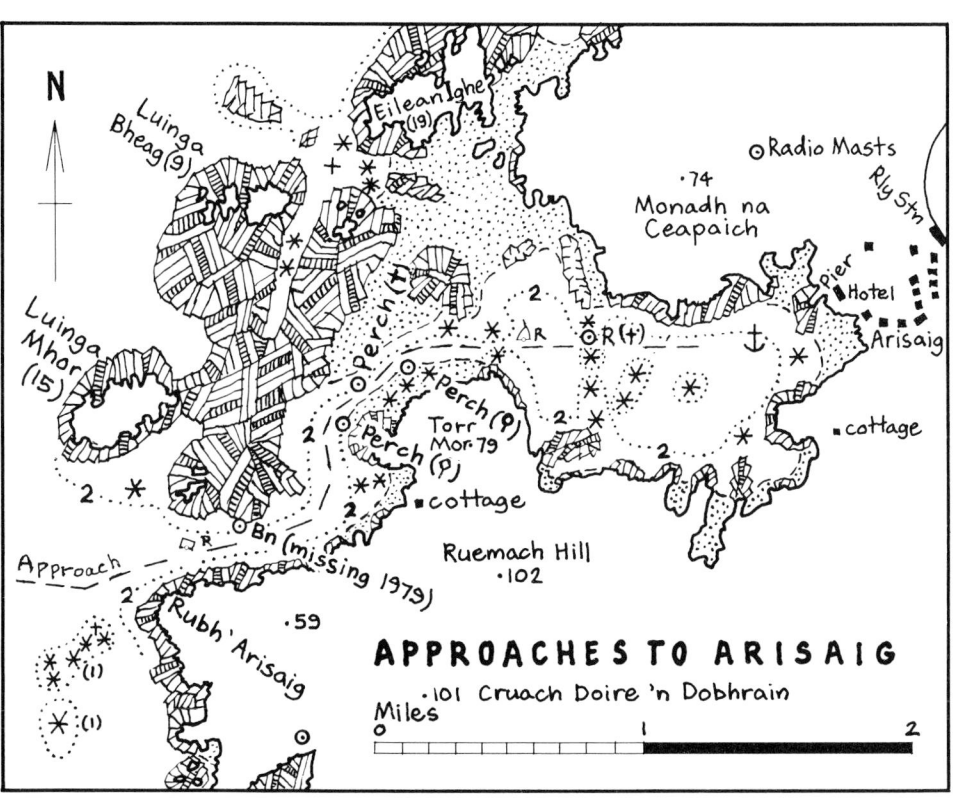

a new arrangement of lights and altering the lines of approach from N and W. The new lights will be finalized and installed in 1986. Details are not yet known, but two new sector lights are being considered, one on the end of the pier.

The approach past Courteachan Point is perfectly easy: coming from the S note that the rocks extend well W of the light beacon N of Rubha na h-Acairseid, so keep at least a cable W of it until it is bearing over 105°Mag., before turning to pass 100m N of it and then curving SE into the harbour.

Anchor *well* S of the line of the outer limb of the Fish Pier, in about 4m; mud, sand and weed. A tripping line is vital here as the bottom is foul: keep it inboard or someone will almost certainly pick it up round their propeller and tow you away. Swinging room is very restricted.

Water from hose, fuel from lorries; there is usually room to go alongside on the Fish Pier, preferably in the morning. Do not leave the boat tied along-side unattended for more than a *very* brief time, in case you have to move her or re-berth. Chandlers, hotels (but remember that in this part of the world, you should be in well before 8 p.m. if you want to get dinner). Excellent shopping; altogether one of the best stocking-up places on this coast.

2 MALLAIG TO LOCH GAIRLOCH, PASSING EAST OF SKYE

Passage notes
The first problem on the way N along the Sound of Sleat is the speed of the streams through Kyle Rhea (pronounced 'ray'), which attain 8 knots or more at springs and produce some fierce whirlpools. The northbound stream begins 6 hr after HW Ullapool, and the southbound stream at HW Ullapool, but there are considerable eddies, mainly along the E bank of the Kyle during the flood and in Bernera Bay during the ebb. It is also worth getting the tides right for Kyle Akin, as even here rates reach 3 knots, the westbound stream running HW +5 to −4 (Ullapool), and being somewhat faster than the eastbound (−3 to +4). Kyle Rhea, Kyle Akin and Loch Alsh are shown without detail on chart 2209, but all dangers are visible or close inshore as

Looking out from Arisaig Harbour. The unmistakable Sgurr of Eigg, a landmark for the whole area, can be seen beyond Luinga Mhor.

Mallaig from the N. The lighthouse can just be seen on the point at the right of the picture.

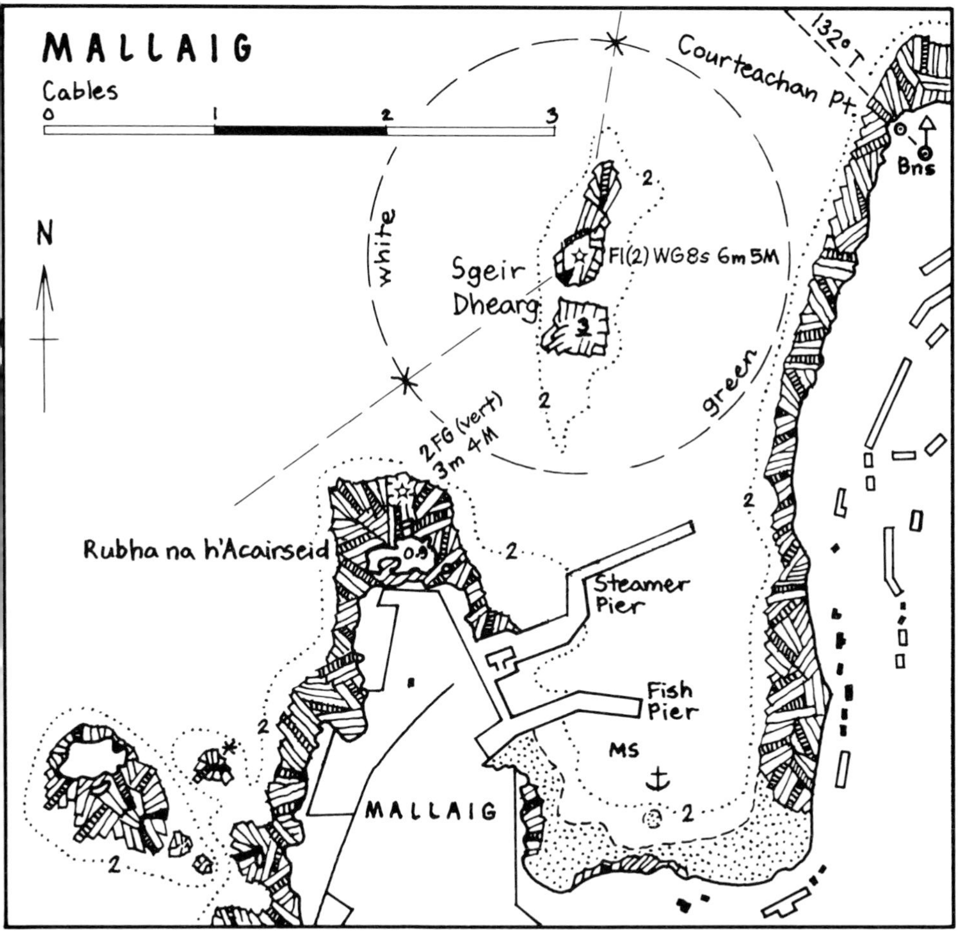

MALLAIG

Cables

Courteachan Pt.

132°T

Bns

white

Sgeir Dhearg

Fl(2) WG8s 6m 5M

2

green

N

2FG (vert) 3m 4M

Rubha na h'Acairseid

Steamer Pier

Fish Pier

MS

MALLAIG

The beacon marking the N spit in the narrows of Scalpay. There is less than 1m at LAT. A light (Q) has now been added.

Inner Loch Nevis. Even the Admiralty warn of the violent squalls that can howl down from the mountains.

long as the passage is made N of the islands off Kyle of Lochalsh, so if just passing through the passage can be made safely using only 2208 and 2209. But note that there are extensive shoals between those islands and the Kyle Akin shore.

Once through Kyle Akin, one can pass S of Scalpay: best water in the narrows is about 10m S of the beacon (Q); there is about 1m at LWN, and it virtually dries at LWS. Then on through the Sound of Raasay (note the 0·4m rock, marked by a G con buoy, Fl (2) G 12s, just N of An Aird), or return to the Inner Sound through the Caol Mor. Alternatively one may go straight up the Inner Sound, either through Linne Crowlin or the Caolas Mor. All these routes are clean of dangers and straightforward; the only possible hazard is the rocks that extend about a mile N of Rona, which must be allowed for if crossing N of Rona, say on passage from Portree to Loch Torridon.

To the N of Rona, the protection given by Skye begins to run out, and although the Outer Hebrides are there to break the full Atlantic swell a westerly wind has a fetch of 30 miles or so into Gairloch, so quite large seas can be encountered.

Loch Nevis 57° 02′N, 5° 44′W
Tidal range 4·3m at mean springs, 1·8m at mean neaps
There is a useful anchorage NE of Eilean na Glaschoille, sheltered in all but S winds. The S side of the entrance to the loch is clean: coming from the N, pass W of Eilean Glas and then keep it in line with the land behind so that no clear water is visible between, until Inverie House comes in sight to the E, on the far shore beyond Rubha Raonuill. These transits clear the dangerous Bogha cas Sruth (dries 1·8m). Then leave to port Bogha Don and Sgeirean Glasa, both marked by beacons, and anchor NE of Glaschoille as close in as soundings and swinging room allow. Sand and mud. No supplies.

The upper part of the loch is subject to very violent squalls from unpredictable directions, and it would be unwise to explore it without reliable power. To pass through the narrows keep along the shore E of Torr an Albannaich about a cable off, easing N a little while passing the first white cottage. From abreast of the second white cottage, steer for the grey ruined cottage E of the long white house on the N shore. From here, steer 30m off the N shore until abreast of Ru Torr na Cartach, then steer to pass just N of the islet off the first point along the S shore, thus avoiding Bogha an Tachard. Then keep in the middle, and anchor N or SE of Eilean Maol as conditions require. This is a difficult passage and should be made with caution, sounding continuously and with a lookout forward. The holding is good, mud and sand, but the head of the loch shoals steeply so do not try to go too far. No supplies.

Isleornsay 57° 09′N, 5° 48′W
Tidal range 4·3m mean springs, 1·6m mean neaps
An unusually easy anchorage to enter: you just sail round the N side of Ornsay, whose offlying reef is marked by a light beacon, and keep going W for the shore, turning S into the anchorage when a cable off the mainland of Skye. Sound carefully as the head of the bay dries a very long way out. Good holding in sand, with little weed. Good shelter except in NE winds when it is uncomfortable rather than dangerous, but it can be a long row to get ashore,

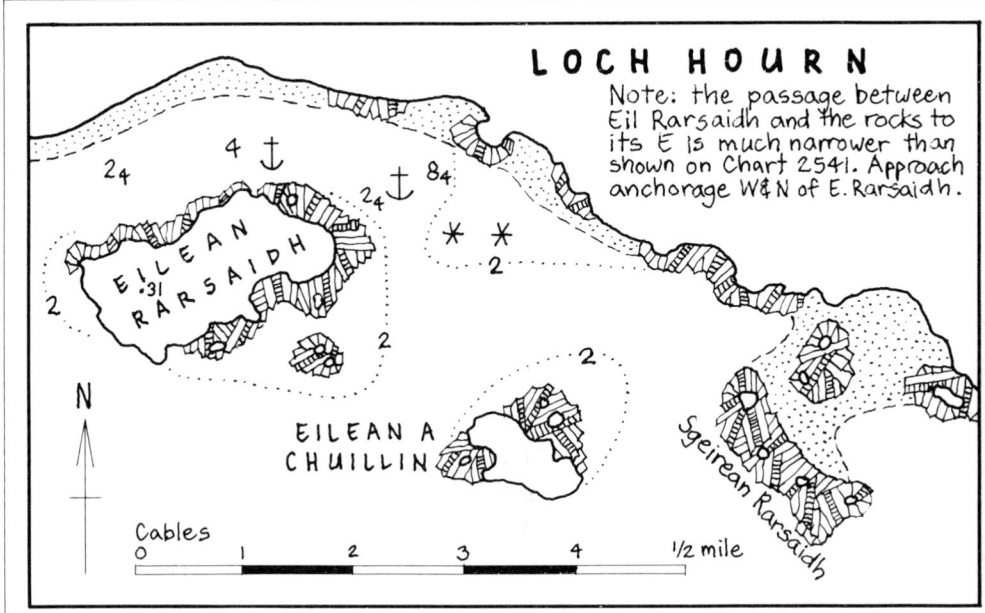

especially at springs when you must anchor even further out, and the passage in the dinghy can be choppy.

The pleasant Hotel Eilean Iarmain does lunches and dinners (7.30 to 8.30) for chance visitors, and bar snacks at lunchtime; baths by arrangement. There is a petrol pump, with a water tap opposite, but the latter is so low to the ground that it is difficult to fill a jerrycan. Telephone box above the hill.

Loch Hourn   (see plan)   57° 09′N, 5° 37′W
To explore the whole of this loch chart 2541 is needed, but the most useful anchorage is near the entrance, and can be reached with chart 2208, using the plan here. Anchor N or E of Eilean Rarsaidh, as conditions require: if going round to the E, keep fairly close to the visible rocks off the E point of the island to avoid the drying shoal lying further E. Approach through the narrow channel N of Rarsaidh. Anchor in 3–6m. No supplies.

Armed with Chart 2541, there is no great difficulty in sailing up the whole of Loch Hourn. Ellice Shoal is best avoided by passing N of Corr Eileanan and S of the islet off A' Chiste Dhubh. Pass through the first narrows close S of Eilean a Gharb-lain, and through the second 100m off the S shore. The only remaining problem is the narrow channel into Loch Beag, which must be followed by sounding. One may anchor in the W part of Camas Ban (good shop, only open in summer), in Poll a' Mhuineil (subject to bad squalls), or in perfect shelter in Loch Beag.

Avernish Bay, Loch Alsh   57° 16½′N, 5° 34¾′W
Charts 2540 and 2541 are needed for this anchorage, which is in the bay just

Avernish Bay. The good holding balances the rather exposed position.

W of Rubh' an Aisig. It is open to the SW, but I have ridden out a force 6 from that quarter safely though uncomfortably: a full gale from the SW would probably be unsafe. Anchor in the middle of the bay in 2–3m, sand and light weed. The path to the road is to the right (E) of the wall of Avernish House, the conspicuous white building near the shore. Land at the E end of the beach: the shingle is finer there. P.O. and telephone at Nostie, but no shop.

Loch Alsh is short of good anchorages. Totaig is much recommended by the CCC but has very poor holding and is crowded with moorings. The best alternative is probably Kyleakin, below, but there are far better places a few miles further on, no matter which way you are going.

Kyleakin   57° 16½′N, 5° 43′W
There is a small pool inside the pier where it is possible to anchor, but the bottom is foul and it is vital to carry a riding light. One may also be able to spend a night alongside the pier on the S side of the pool, if necessary alongside a fishing boat. I confess I have never done this: it is the sort of crowded and busy place I try to avoid.

Kyle of Lochalsh   57° 17′N, 5° 43′W
Tidal range: 4·5m at mean springs; 1·7m at mean neaps
Unfortunately there is nowhere set aside for yachts in this important railhead and ferry port, but it is often possible to find a temporary berth alongside the E end of the pier. This usually can be kept for long enough to refuel (but beware fast delivery and slow reactions when asked to stop, which can result in five

gallons of diesel oil fountaining up into the air and ending in the bilges). Water by hose, excellent shopping. Kyle is the furthest N of the west coast railway stations, but the line runs NE to Inverness, so is very slow for connections to the south compared with say Mallaig.

Sound of Raasay

At this point on the journey N, two alternatives present themselves: the Sound of Raasay and the Inner Sound. The latter provides the more direct route, but I will deal with the former, which runs up the E side of Skye, first.

Broadford Bay   57° 15′N, 5° 54′W

Tidal range: 4·6m at mean springs, 1·9m at mean neaps

Though a popular anchorage, this is very exposed to the N and NE, and in strong winds from those directions it can become untenable. Approaching from the E keep well towards the Pabay side, as the E side of the bay and its approaches is foul. Note Sgeir Ghobhlach, SW of Pabay and marked by a beacon: from a position 2 cables S of this beacon it is safe to steer for the W shore of the bay and anchor in 5–8m, mud. Beware old timbers off the end of the pier. Stores and hotel in the village. Strollamus Boat Centre (tel Broadford (047 12) 596), 4m N of Broadford Bay opposite Scalpay and just through the Narrows, has moorings and can supply water and diesel by hose, Calor, Camping Gaz, and do boat and engine repairs. The Narrows are buoyed and lit for night approach, but very shallow so do not attempt them before half tide at least.

Loch Ainort   57° 17′N, 6° 03′W

No navigational hazards except near the head, which dries for up to 3 cables. Anchor in 3m near the S shore about 2 cables short of Sron Ard Mhullaich. Severe squalls can come down from the mountains. No facilities.

The Avernish Bay anchorage from offshore

Portree Harbour   57° 25′N, 6° 11′W
Tidal range 4·6m at mean springs, 1·8m at mean neaps
An excellent harbour offering good shelter and all facilities. The loch dries
SW of the line between the two points: anchor NE of the pier and clear of
moorings as space and soundings allow. The N side of the bay dries some way
out, so sound carefully. Fuel, water, all stores and good hotels.

Kyleakin Pool. Lie alongside the pier (left) or to a fishing boat: limited room to
anchor.

The anchorage, Portree

Eilean Fladday   57° 29′N, 6° 01′W
This perfectly protected anchorage lies between Fladday and Raasay, and is completely landlocked, although some swell gets in in strong N to NW winds, when Acairseid Mhor, below, is preferable. The approach from the N is simple, keeping in mid-channel: anchor in 6m where the channel broadens out after the first narrows. (It is also possible to anchor S of them in good holding and sheltered, but approach is much more difficult.) Good holding. There is no passage for a yacht through the second narrows. Chart 2210 gives all the information needed. No facilities, but a charming and pretty place to spend a night.

Acairseid Mhor   (see plan) 57° 32′N, 5° 59′W
A little natural harbour that is perfectly protected, although the entrance can be tricky in heavy weather, or near HW, when the rocks cover. The easiest approach is S and E of Eilean Garbh, the island lying in the entrance of the loch. Approaching from the S there is a white painted arrow visible on the S face of the island, but the W coast of Rona is clean of hazards and there is no problem in identifying the entrance if one keeps close in. Once the harbour opens up through the narrows, continue N until rather nearer the N shore than the S, before curving E and steering to pass 100m off the SE point of the N headland, and then close NW of the inner islet. This avoids the trickiest rock, which lies just S of mid-channel. Keep a lookout in the bows.

From the N, it is vital to keep at least 1½ cables off the islets off the promontory N of the harbour entrance until the N end of Eilean Garbh is bearing E Mag. Then steer to pass 75m N of the N tip of Garbh, S of a group of rocks that only covers at HWS, after which keep 50m off the visible dangers along the N shore and so into the anchorage.

Anchor in 2–3m N of the inner islet (there is a mooring buoy, which may be free): beware the reef that runs out to its E. Or in 8m in the first bay on the S side after passing the mid-channel rock. Do not steer S until E of the southernmost tip of the land on the N side of the harbour. No facilities, but a particularly sheltered and beautiful anchorage.

Staffin Bay   57° 38′N, 6° 13′W
This bay offers good holding in sand and shelter from all but N winds. Anchor at the E or W side of the bay according to wind; do not go S of the S end of Staffin Island at the E side, as there is a shallow bank. Shop, hotel.

Kilmaluag Bay   57° 41½′N, 6° 18′W
This bay is completely open to NE and E, but is a most useful temporary anchorage, for instance to wait for a W gale to blow itself out before rounding the N of Skye, or before leaving the shelter of the island going N. Keep well off the S shore on the approach, as a long drying reef projects N from it; otherwise there are no hazards. Anchor near the head of the bay, 3–4m, sand. No supplies. On no account leave a boat unattended, or sleep without an anchor watch, if there is the slightest risk of the wind coming round into the E as the bay is then very dangerous.

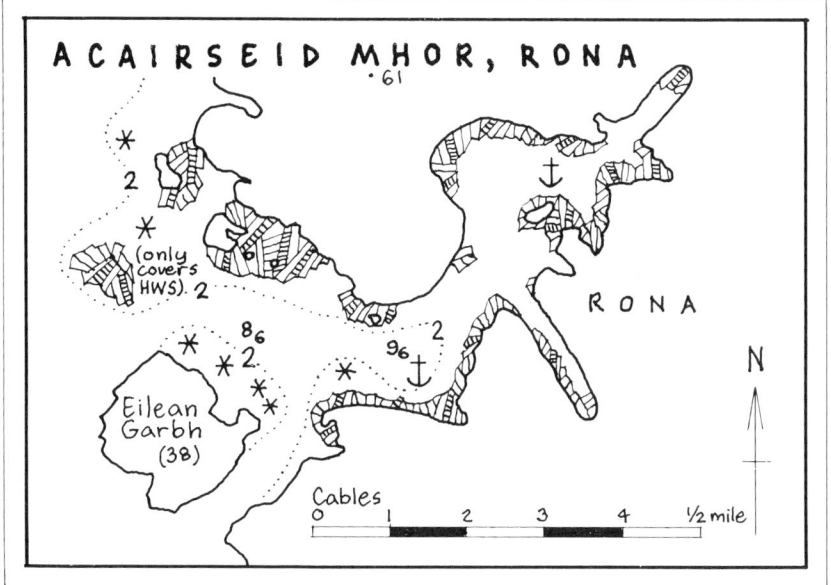

A CAIRSEID MHOR, RONA

The Inner Sound
This provides the main route from Loch Alsh to the north.

Plockton   57° 20′N, 5° 39′W
Tidal range 3·7m at mean springs, 1·9m at mean neaps
Chart 2528 is useful but not strictly necessary for entering Loch Carron. Pass
between Sgeir Bhuidhe (unnamed on 2209, but shown as 4m high with light
Fl 3s) and Sgeir Golach, the rocks 4 cables to the SSE, which cover just above
half-tide and are marked by a green beacon with a N cone (Fl G 3s). From N
of the Golach beacon, steer to pass 3 cables E of it, and then steer to pass 1
cable E of Rubha Mor and so into the bay, keeping well over to the W side to
avoid the spit of rocks NW of Duncraig Castle. Anchor in mud as space
allows, clear of permanent moorings. Sound carefully: the head of the bay
dries, and both sides are shoal. All stores, hotels etc; considerable yachting
development; small boat and Windsurfer hire and instruction.

Slumbay Harbour, Loch Carron   57° 23′N, 5° 30′W
The channel from Plockton up to the narrows is buoyed, and presents little
difficulty. The tide runs at 2 knots in the narrows at Strome. Slumbay
Harbour lies N of Slumbay Island (actually a peninsula) and can be approached direct except at LW, passing close W of Sgeir Chreagach to avoid
the dangerous Red Rock, then steering NW for 2 cables before turning WSW
and sounding into the bay. Anchor in 2–3m, mud and sand. At LWS it is
necessary to pass E of Sgeir Chreagach and through the channel between it
and Sgeir Fhada to the NE.
   Shops, hotel at Lochcarron village, trains to Inverness from Strathcarron,
4 miles away.

Loch Kishorn   57° 23′N, 5° 38′W

A good anchorage on passage is to be found E of Kishorn Island. Approaching from the N there are no hazards; anchor E of the island in 5–6m. In SW gales better shelter can be found NE of the Grarra Islands, $3\frac{1}{2}$m, but careful sounding is needed to get far enough S to find shelter without getting among the rocks as the bottom shoals suddenly. No facilities, and noisy as oil rigs are constructed on the loch. Beware unlit mooring buoys.

Crowlin Island   57° 21′N, 5° 51′W

Chart 2209 does scant justice to this, one of my favourite anchorages, which has water much further in than indicated. The anchorage lies between Eilean Meadhonach and Eilean Mor, and is approached from the N, E of Eilean Beg (lighthouse). Keeping to mid-channel, there is 1·7m as far as the point where the low cliff on the starboard (W) side gives way to stony beach. This is already S of where the chart shows the drying line. It gives shelter from all but strong northerly winds and is a perfectly good place for a short stay. But a channel drying 0·1m at LAT, thus having $2\frac{1}{2}$m or more at half-tide, leads S through into an inner pool with $3\frac{1}{2}$m at LAT, perfectly sheltered. If trying this inner pool, keep rather to the W side of mid-channel. There is no way in or out from the S. No facilities, but perfect peace and the chance of a visiting seal. Reasonable holding, but I would want lines ashore to weather a full-scale northerly gale.

Poll Domhain   (see plan)   57° 23½′N, 5° 49′W

This pleasant deserted anchorage is sheltered from all but NW winds. The rocks W of the Ardban peninsula are marked by a beacon: give the point a good berth to the N, and enter keeping a little W of mid-channel. Good holding, and a nice shingle beach, but do not risk it if there is a danger of strong norwesterlies. Very little swinging room: do not go too far in.

Slumbay Harbour anchorage, Loch Carron

Poll Creadha   (see plan)   57° 24′N, 5° 48½′W
A tricky entrance, not for the inexperienced. Strangers, however skilled, should make their first visit in moderate weather and good visibility, using the NW entrance although the SW one has a lot to be said for it once you know the place.

To approach from the NW, make a position between Eilean nan Naomh and the W point of the mainland to the N. Looking SE from here, the leading marks (white painted posts) may be seen below the second white cottage from the left. If not, then as long as the conspicuous wreck is still there, steer for a position about 100m W of it. From here the leading marks should certainly be seen. The channel is marked by beacons, but these were thin and rusty in 1979. Once inside, turn up the line of moorings and anchor where space allows, clear of them. Perfect shelter except in northerlies near HWS, when the rocks cover and swell can become heavy. Shop at Camusterrach.

Coming out by the SW passage (6m at LWS), two beacons N of Aird-dubh are left 100m to port, and then the one at the end of the long reef running S from Eilean nan Naomh is left 50m to starboard; then steer W into open water. Do not go too far off the last beacon, as it is only 200m from Seal Rock to the SSE. This passage is in fact the better of the two in winds from N to W, but only when it is known as the beacons, which are the only man-made marks, are thin and difficult to see so one must recognise the rocks and islets.

Loch a'Chracaich, Loch Torridon   57° 33′N, 5° 44′W
The S side of the entrance to Loch Torridon is foul and must be given a berth of at least ¾ mile. Approaching Loch a' Chracaich, rocks run out from the point to its N for nearly 400m. Round these, and anchor in the NW corner of the loch off Kenmore. The shore shelves steeply, so anchor in no less than 10m. Coming from the N the problem of where to steer for is solved by

Crowlin Island: entrance to anchorage

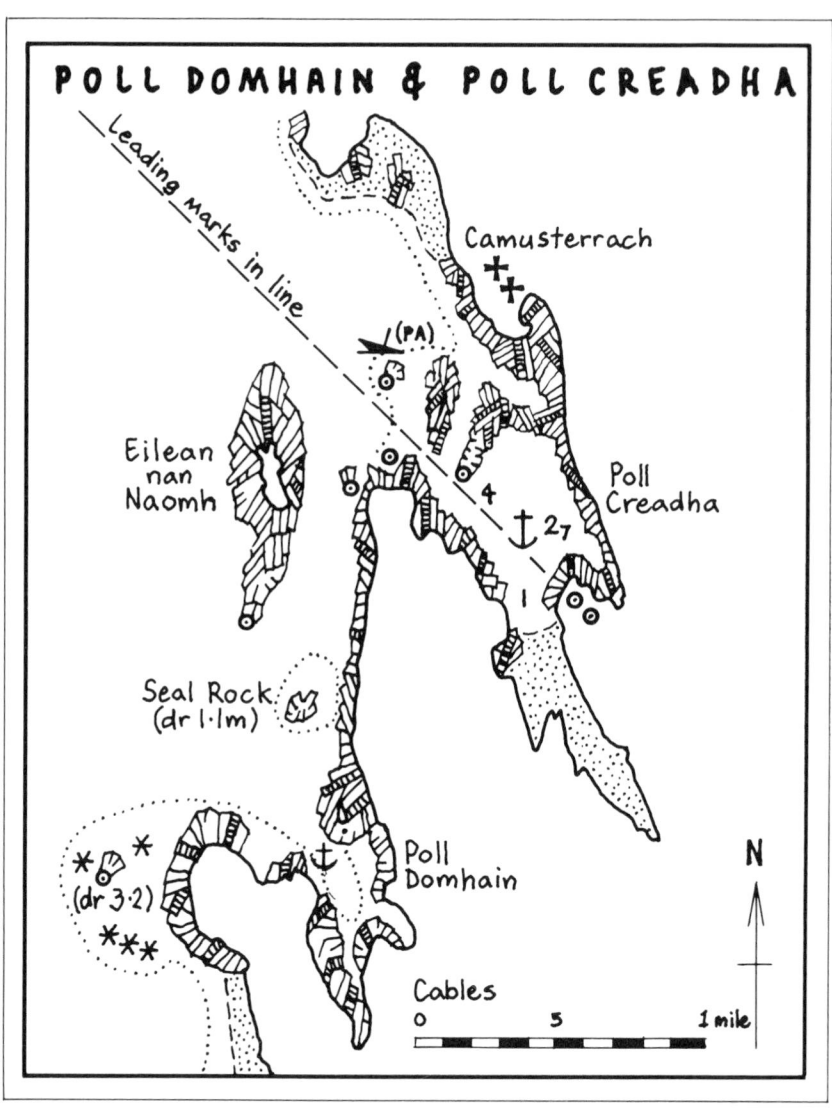

POLL DOMHAIN & POLL CREADHA

Leading marks in line

Camusterrach

(PA)

Eilean
nan
Naomh

Poll
Creadha

4

2₇

Seal Rock.
(dr 1·1m)

(dr 3·2)

Poll
Domhain

N

Cables

0   5   1 mile

keeping the E side of Sgeir na Trian in line with the end of Red Point. No
facilities, but pretty and well sheltered.

Loch Shieldaig, Loch Torridon   57° 31½′N, 5° 39′W
Tidal range: 4.9m at mean springs, 2·0m at mean neaps
There is excellent anchorage in all but NW winds E of Shieldaig Island, but
it is essential not to go too far S. A bar of rock runs across from the village
to the SE part of the island, and this all but dries. Anchor in no less than 3½m
LAT, as the holding further S becomes progressively worse. In the right place
(the War Memorial N of the village bearing E Mag.) holding is good, weed

Poll Creadha. Leave the wreck lying on the shoal 100m to port going in.

Loch a' Chracaich. Anchor behind the point in perfect shelter, though rather deep.

Loch Shieldaig, Loch Torridon. Anchor E (left) of the islet on the right of the picture.

and mud. Two shops, P.O., hotel with restaurant but no bar licence, open 10–5 and 7–9. They welcome yachtsmen, but meals must be finished by the later times given owing to staff shortages. Good supplies.

Upper Loch Torridon   57° 32′N, 5° 32′W
The narrows into the Upper Loch are free from hazards, but the tide runs through at 2–3 knots, and with some overfalls from a very uneven bottom there can be quite a nasty sea with wind over tide. The best anchorage in fair weather is at the SE end of the loch, 1½ cable N of the slip W of the hotel; 3m, sand and weed. The deep bay W of Sron an Dubh-Aird gives better shelter in E winds; anchor near its head in 3½m.

Loch Gairloch   57° 43′N, 5° 45′W
The main loch is wide and faces the W with a clear fetch of over 30 miles from Harris, so quite a sea can roll in in bad weather. Fortunately, though, there are two perfectly sheltered anchorages. Badachro (see plan) lies to the W of Eilean Horrisdale on the S side of the loch. Enter keeping close along the island (E) side, and anchor S of a lone rock marked by a perch. All to the W of here is full of moorings, and shallow. Badachro Inn in the village not only welcomes yachtsmen, but there are plans for moorings, fuel supply and a slipway. P.O./shop.

Loch Shieldaig, at the SE end of Loch Gairloch (not to be confused with the one in Loch Torridon, already described), can be entered without difficulty using chart 2210. Keep over to the E side and anchor E of the more southerly of the two islands in 3½m, mud. Buoy the anchor, as there are some mooring chains on the bottom. Hotel.

3 MALLAIG TO LOCH GAIRLOCH PASSING WEST OF SKYE

Passage notes

This passage provides some of the wildest and grandest scenery in the whole of our area, but it must be emphasised that the weather can be pretty wild and grand too, and no yacht should venture out to the W coast of Skye unless its crew are confident of their ability to cope with heavy seas, strong streams and tide-rips, and to stay at sea if the visibility closes down at an inconvenient moment.

Ports of refuge are sheltered but widely spaced, usually separated by head-lands with more or less severe races off their ends: these get progressively

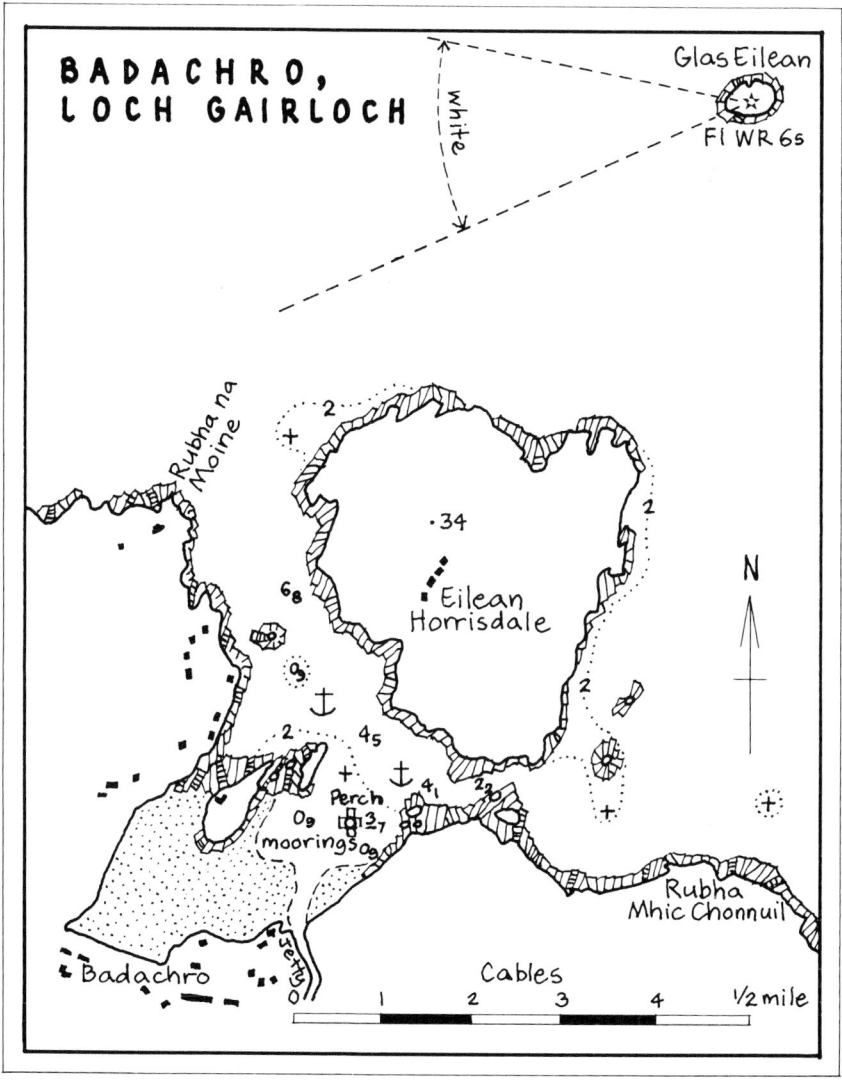

Badachro, Loch Gairloch. Anchor to the right of the picture or beyond the spit: the main foreground has less than 1m average depth.

more severe towards the N. The main offshore dangers are the mile-long reef projecting S from the shore halfway between Hoe and Idrigill Points, W of Loch Bracadale: luckily there is a skerry at the end of the reef that never covers. There are passages through the reef easily found near LW, but I would not advise using them except in fair weather with little swell. Off Rubha Hunish, the more westerly of the twin N points of Skye, strong tide eddies and overfalls can be encountered, which for some reason are unmarked on the chart although they can be as bad as any that are. This can be a dangerous area in fog, because of the extensive reef in mid-channel between Fladda-chuain and Eilean Trodday onto which the tide sets at up to 2½ knots in the three hours before local HW. Once E of Trodday, the passage across to the mainland and Loch Gairloch is straightforward.

Loch Eishort   57° 10′N, 5° 56′W

I mention this loch mainly to warn against it. The entrance is tricky above half-tide, when many of the outer rocks cover. A perfectly straight line from close S of the mid-channel skerry (the one whose position is given at the top of this entry) to Sgeir Gormul, turning at the last moment to leave the latter 50m to port, clears the shoal that dries 0·3m, after which a line 50m off the visible dangers along the S shore is safe until the bay behind

Neist Point and lighthouse, West Skye

McLeod's Maidens, a landmark on the W coast of Skye

Eilean Heast opens up, when it is safe to steer NW into it (but not before it is fully open: the white house on the foreshore should be entirely clear of the end of the island).

This is tricky enough, and note that at high springs the mid-channel skerry and Sgeir Gormul both cover and the entrance then becomes almost impossible. But the real problem is the holding. The best place to anchor is at the W side of the bay, close under the island, but the bottom everywhere is soft silty mud, and in a quite moderate gale I have pulled two CQRs, totalling 60lb, through it like a knife through butter. Shelter from sea is perfect, but the island is low and gives no lee from the wind, so if any reader ignores my advice and visits the loch he would be well advised to do so in moderate weather at half-tide, and take a line ashore.

Loch Slapin   57°12'N, 6° 01'W
The loch must be entered keeping well over to the W side, but not so close as to risk fouling the drying rocks $\frac{1}{2}$ mile S of the narrows. Anchor on the W side of the loch in 5m, about 250m N of the narrows. Moderate holding in soft mud. The head of the loch dries for $\frac{1}{2}$ mile. There is excellent shelter in W or NW winds, but severe swell gets in if the sea is running from the S, or even SW. No stores. Water tap on the shore S of the anchorage.

Loch Scavaig   57° 12'N, 6° 10'W
Undoubtedly this is one of the most spectacular anchorages in our area, fully comparable with some of the most dramatic on the W coast of Norway. There are many rocks, but the entrance presents no great difficulty though it requires steady nerves.

Approach up the W side of the loch, steering to give Eilean Reamhar a berth of 20m near HW; a little less near LW. From here steer for the W end of Eilean Glas, the island at the NW end of the loch. (It appears as two on the chart, but seldom looks that way, and never from the approach.) At HWS, when the reef midway between Reamhar and Glas covers, keep just to E of the direct line in that area: the shoal is just S of where the shore bears sharply to the W.

There is a rock off the W end of the island, and by an optical illusion there often appears to be more room to pass W and N of the rock, but do not do so. Pass between the rock and the island, and anchor N of the island. The drying rock W of Glas seldom covers: if it is, creep in as close to Glas as soundings and nerves allow, with a lookout in the bow. Holding is poor in soft mud and squalls can be violent, so it is advisable to take a line to the weather shore; but there is perfect shelter from sea. No supplies, but not to be missed. Do not, however, be lulled into a sense of false security if the wind is from the N: squalls can roar down from the mountain without warning out of a clear sky.

Soay Harbour   57° 09$\frac{1}{2}$'N, 6° 13'W
Tidal range 4·1m at mean springs, 1·7m at mean neaps
A narrow creek on the N side of Soay. The bar dries right across about $\frac{1}{2}$m at MLWS; otherwise chart 2208 gives an accurate picture. Enter and leave only within 2 hr of HW, when there is over 3m on the bar: keep right in the middle of the channel and sound carefully. Anchor beyond the bar but no more

Pass between the rocks and the W end of Eilean Glas (right of picture) to enter the anchorage of Loch Scavaig. (Alas, it was pouring with rain when I took the picture.)

than 100m beyond the derelict building on the E shore; good holding. Sometimes there is a little swell reflected from the Skye shore near HW.

Loch Harport   57° 20′N, 6° 26′W
There are no problems entering this loch, and there is a good light on Ardtreck Point. However, do give the point a good berth near HW as covering rocks run out further than the chart shows. A useful anchorage in the dark is just E of the spit joining Oronsay to Skye, as it can be found by making a position W of Ardtreck light, and then keeping it bearing E Mag. astern until the water shallows enough to anchor. There is some swell.

Loch Beag is crowded with moorings and subject to swell, and the best anchorage is off Carbost, near the head of Loch Harport. There is good holding in stiff mud, no weed, about 100m beyond the Tallisker distillery. This is the only distillery on Skye and well worth a visit. There is an inn, a small shop and a P.O. No bread, no meat. Arrowspeed Transport may be able to help with engine repairs.

Loch Dunvegan   57° 26′N, 6° 35′W
Tidal range 4·5m at mean springs, 1·7m at mean neaps
Large-scale chart 2533 should be aboard if it is intended to visit any of the numerous secondary anchorages among the islands at the head of the loch. However, chart 1795 is quite adequate for the main anchorage at Dunvegan.

Keep midway between Fiadhairt, the first major peninsula on the NE shore, and the islet 4 cables to the SW of it; from there leave Uignish Point 1 cable to starboard and so proceed up the loch, anchoring off the hotel jetty or as

Wiay Island, with its spectacular sea caves in the entrance to Loch Harport.

The anchorage off Carbost, Loch Harport

Uig Bay, Loch Snizort. Anchor behind the pier, which breaks the swell.

soundings allow. Good holding in clean mud. Safe in all winds, though some swell gets in in strong NW winds.

The hotel, run by Iain and Sandra Houston, not only does meals and bar snacks but has locker rooms and showers specially for yachtsmen. Shops include a baker, rare in these parts, but no meat or bank. Delicious mussels for the gathering, though: mind your teeth on the pearls! Dunvegan Castle, which is open to the public, has been the home of successive McLeods of Dunvegan for seven centuries.

Other anchorages that can be reached using only chart 1795 are S of Eilean Mor, the more easterly of the two large islands in the bay W of Uiginish Point; and for a rest while on passage, Ardmore Bay at the N entrance of the loch, moderate holding on stony bottom in 5m about where the ring of the Admiralty anchor symbol is drawn on chart 1795. No stores at either. The anchorage S of Eilean Mor would be the best if a bad nor'wester was expected; good holding in mud and shell.

Uig Bay, Loch Snizort   57° 35′N, 6° 22′W
Here too chart 2533 provides large-scale coverage but no extra information. Approach the pierhead from SW Mag. to avoid the extensive shoal projecting from the shore to the W of it, and anchor about 150m N of the pierhead in 3m, mud. The head of the bay dries extensively. It is exposed to the SW, but the pier structure takes the weight out of the sea. Diesel and water at the pier: contact West Highland Salmon Fisheries at the large white house with dormer windows near the root of the pier. They also have limited chandlery. The Ferry Inn will supply baths and are helpful. Shops, baker, P.O.

Loch Snizort Beag   57° 29′N, 6° 19½′W

In strong SW winds, when Uig Bay is uncomfortable, total shelter can be found in Loch Snizort Beag 6 miles to the S, in the middle of the three branches into which the loch divides. Keep over towards the W side when entering this branch, and anchor in 2m, mud, 1 cable off the W shore; Dun Fada, the middle and highest of the three peaks will be bearing E Mag. Shop and P.O. in Bernisdale village SW of the anchorage.

There are no anchorages between Uig Bay and Loch Gairloch except Kilmaluag Bay and Staffin Bay on the NE coast of Skye, which were covered in the section above on the Sound of Raasay.

4 LOCH GAIRLOCH TO ULLAPOOL AND THE SUMMER ISLES

Passage notes

The navigation for this last leg of our journey is perfectly straightforward. Tidal streams are barely perceptible and there are no offshore dangers near the direct passage; the only possible worry is that the coast is totally unprotected from the N and very high seas are experienced during northerly gales, and quite severe ones in NW or W gales. Shelter is never far away, however, so the cruising yachtsman who listens to the forecasts is unlikely to experience any problems.

Loch Ewe   57° 50′N, 5° 36′W
Tidal range 4·4m at mean springs, 1·8m at mean neaps

There are no sunken hazards to yachts in the loch except for the rocks in the W part of Poolewe Bay and the drying sands along the shores, but there are numerous unlit mooring and other buoys so navigation in the dark can be hazardous. In all but S winds, one of the best anchorages is in line and about midway between the jetty on Aird Point and the Aultbea Hotel jetty, 4m, mud. Aird Point is not named on chart 1794 but it is the long headland W of the hotel, E of the Isle of Ewe. All stores in the village.

In S or SW winds, a more comfortable berth is at the extreme S end of the loch, in the W part of Poolewe Bay. Keep to the middle until nearing the S shore to avoid Boor Rocks (though the main ones never cover) and anchor 200m offshore a cable E of the southernmost point of the bay, or in E winds further E and further offshore with the conspicuous hotel bearing no more than 150°Mag. Good holding in stiff mud; I found no weed. Hotel, shop, P.O. Bus to Inverness (0745 or 0815 according to day of week: check at the hotel), so it can be a convenient point for changing crews in the far north.

Loch Thurnaig, Loch Ewe   57° 47½′N, 5° 36′W
The anchorage is in the extreme SW corner of the loch, protected by a rock spit that covers at HW and projects from the N shore of the SW arm. This is clearly marked in miniature even on chart 1794, and the large-scale chart is not really necessary.

Enter Loch Thurnaig down its W shore, which is clean, and pass N and W of the floating pontoons with huts on them that are moored in the mouth of

Approaching Poolewe, Loch Ewe

Loch Thurnaig, Loch Ewe. Pass to right (NW) of the rafts, then cross to the S to avoid the spit.

the SW extension of the loch. From here steer 200°Mag. until 50m off the S shore and turn W along it. Near LW, when the whole of the reef from the N shore is visible, steer to pass midway between its end and the S shore, and then turn N along the moorings and anchor to the N of them. If the reef is covered keep 50m off the S shore until in line with the moorings, and only then turn N. No supplies.

Laide Bay, Gruinard Bay. Anchor below the long white bungalow (centre).

Gruinard Bay   57° 52′N, 5° 32′W
The anchorage here is in Laide Bay, sheltered except from N and NE. Gruinard Island in the middle of the bay is infected with anthrax as a result of wartime experiments, and landing is strictly prohibited, not to mention unwise.

Laide Bay has a stretch of white sand and a road running down to the beach, but note that Udrigill Bay, a mile to the N, has an exactly similar combination of features. Having identified the bay (from which the summit of Gruinard Island bears 70°Mag.) approach from N of W Mag. as there is a long drying spit at the E end of the bay. Look out for keep nets off the salmon hut, and anchor below the long white bungalow in 3m. Stony holding. Avoid in N to NE winds, and in strong easterlies, but it is a good place to ride out a westerly blow. Do not be tempted by the nice looking sandy bay to the SE: it is rocky and shoal offshore. Shop, P.O.

The Summer Isles
If it is intended to explore this wonderful archipelago fully, chart 2501 should be carried, but for the anchorages below 1794 is enough. This is the most northerly point in the coverage of this book, and on June 20 the sun rises over the islands at 0416 BST and sets at 2226, so with more than an hour of twilight at each end of the day there is very little real night.

Isle Ristol   58° 02½′N, 5° 25½′W
Excellent anchorage can be found in the channel from the S between the island and the mainland. Take the narrows in mid-channel, then keep 100m off the E shore and anchor before the bay opens up on the E side: beyond this line it is shoal. Some lop in strong S winds.

Tanera Beg   (see plan)   58° 01′N, 5° 27′W
This anchorage is most easily approached from the W, passing midway between Eilean a Char and Tanera Beg, then turning S and keeping close

down the E shore of Tanera Beg; or from the N, turning sharp W immediately S of Eilean Choinaid and then curving S into the anchorage (see plan). It can also be approached from the S, but only at half-tide, taking care to avoid the drying rock right in the middle of the S part of the channel, by keeping well to the W of mid-channel until clear of it. Just N of this a reef (not shown on chart 2501) projects from Tanera Beg, and it is necessary to move out nearly but not quite to mid-channel. Readers attempt this difficult channel at their own risk.

The anchorage is in a perfectly sheltered lagoon between Tanera Beg and Eilean Fada Mor. In fine weather one can anchor in the middle in 10–12m, sand, but in strong N winds this can be uncomfortable and it is better to tuck in to the bay to the W. Note that the reef marked on the plan (and see photo) is not shown at all fully on chart 2501. No supplies, landing difficult except at HW.

Tanera More   (see plan)   58° 01′N, 5° 24′W
Tidal range 4·3m at mean springs, 1·9m at mean neaps
The best known anchorage is in the large bay on the E side of the island, close in near the pier in 10m, or in better shelter in the bay S of the channel between Eilean Mor and Eilean Beg, 6–7, mud. Water and diesel are available at the new pier.

My favourite anchorage, however, is at the NW corner of the island, in

The W anchorage on Tanera Beg near LWS. The drying spit is not marked on chart 2501.

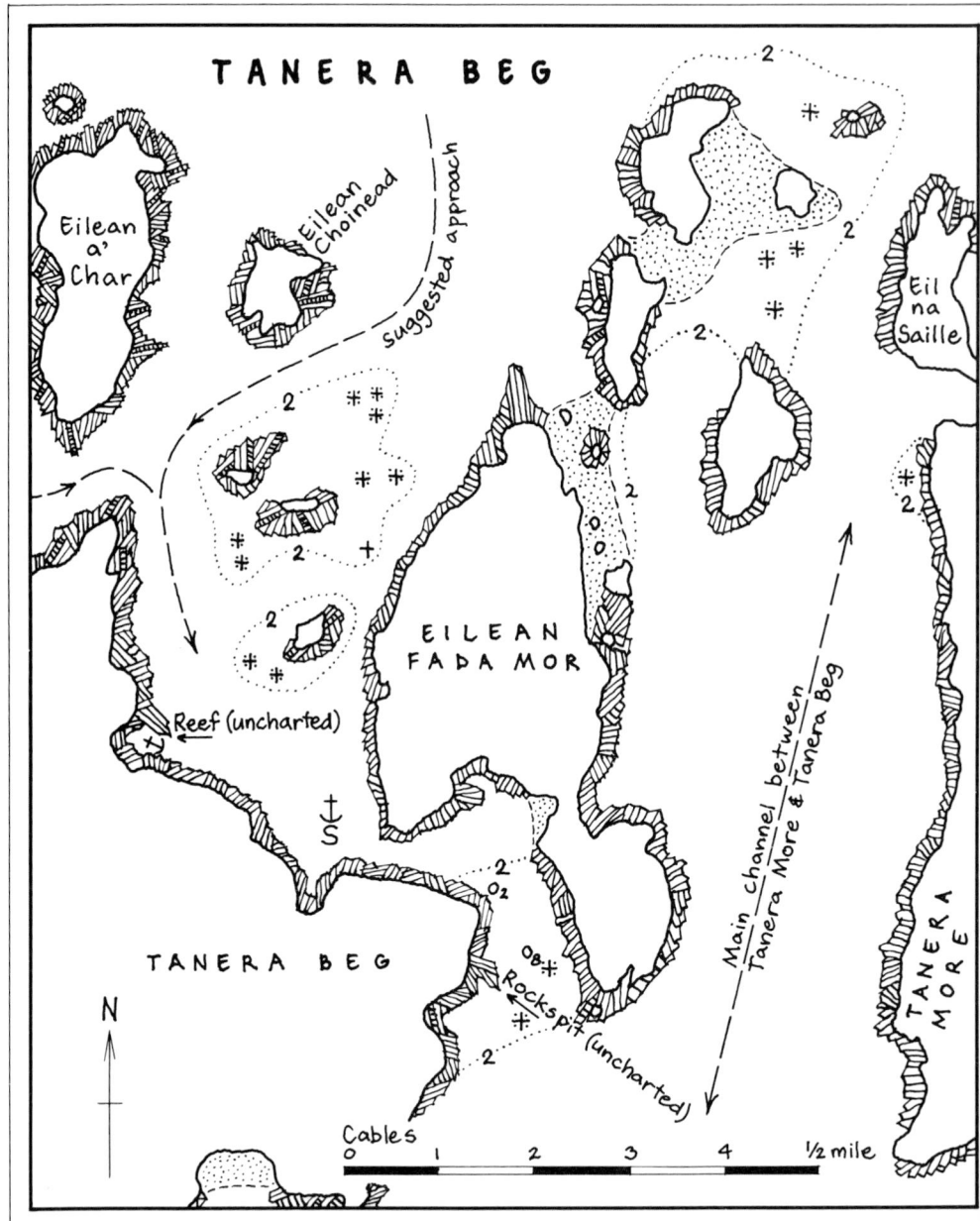

TANERA BEG

Eilean a' Char

Eilean Choinead

Suggested approach

Eil na Saille

2

2

2

2

2

2

2

2

2

EILEAN FADA MOR

Reef (uncharted)

⚓
S

Main channel between Tanera More & Tanera Beg

2

2
O₂

O8

Rockspit (uncharted)

2

TANERA BEG

TANERA MORE

N

Cables
0   1   2   3   4   ½ mile

the bay E of Eilean na Saille. Do not go too far in as there is a drying rock in the middle of the bay which is steep-to and so gives little warning from soundings. Anchor in 3½m in the middle, just S of E from the NE point of na Saille, and 50m before the bay widens out on the port (E) side. Sand and weed. Slight swell in N winds. No supplies or population.

Horse Island   57° 59′N, 5° 21′W
There is good anchorage in the bay to the E of Horse Island and Meall nan Gabhar, the island to its N. Keep in the N half of the bay as there is an uncharted reef in the S part, and anchor in 3m, sand and some weed. Exposed to E. No stores.

Little Loch Broom   57° 51′N, 5° 15′W
This loch has steep-to shores and is subject to violent squalls. There is no really good anchorage, but it is possible to get some shelter E of Camus-nagaul, on the S shore near the head of the loch (which dries for ½ mile). Anchor in 3–5m, sand and mud. There is swell if the wind is blowing up the loch. Shop, P.O. Hotel a mile away at Dundonnell, at the head of the loch.

Loch Kanaird   57° 56½′N, 5° 12′W
A fascinating pool that is almost cut off to the S by a reef that runs across from Isle Martin to the mainland, but there is a narrow pass through the middle with 2·2m in it. The chart gives a transit which is impossible to make out in my experience. Instead, keep the NE point of Martin in line with a whitish rock at the bottom of a leftward-leaning diagonal on the cliff to N; this does very well as a leading line. Or simply approach Rubha Giubhais (the NE point of Martin) on exactly true N (say 11°Mag.). The entry round the N of Isle Martin from the W is straightforward. Anchor at the S end of the bay S of Rubha Giubhais in 5–7m, mud. No supplies.

Little Loch Broom

Ullapool   57° 53½′N, 5° 09′W

I chose Ullapool as the finishing point for this book because it is by far the largest town in the area, and it has relatively good communications by bus with Inverness and so can be used reasonably conveniently for changing crews. Of course there are beautiful places further N, but as Mr Plimsoll remarked, you have to draw the line somewhere.

The approach up Loch Broom is straightforward, just taking care at HW to keep SW of the lit buoy (QR) marking the extensive shoal W of Ullapool Point. There are now many moorings in the bay. One may be available: if not, anchor to the E of them, 8m, sand. Water and diesel are available on the pier, but it is badly adapted for yachts and is positively dangerous in strong onshore winds. I have seen a yacht badly damaged by a night alongside. There is also a water tap at the back of the brown wooden office of the garage just at the root of the landing slip, E of the pier. Good shops, hotels and restaurants; chandler with good range of equipment; and a launderette in the street parallel with the sea front but one back. Baths at the Caledonian Hotel by arrangement. Repairs can be organized by the chandlers, or during the week Summer Isles Charters at Altnaharrie Inn on the opposite side of the loch may be able to help. Moorings, water and diesel (not weekends), also good food.

Ullapool

Notes on Gaelic

Pronunciation

Bh or **Mh** is pronounced **V. Fh** is mute. **C** is always hard, as **K**. At the end of a word **-aidh** is pronounced as the **y** in **my**, **-idh** as the **y** in **ferry**. In the middle of a word **ea** is usually spoken as the **e** in **well**, **ao** as the **oo** in **pool**.

Meanings

Acairseid	Anchorage	Glas	Grey, Green
Aline	Meadow, green place	Gleann	Valley
Aird, Ard	Promontory	Gorm, Ghorm	Blue-green
Bagh, Baigh	Bay	Innis, Inch	Island
Ban	Fair, white (also woman)	Inver	Mouth of river
		Kyle (as Caol)	Strait
Beg, Beag	Small	Leac	Scree
Bogha, Bodha (pron. Boa, Voa)	Covering rock	Liath	Grey
Buidhe, Bhuide (pron. Buie, Vuie)	Yellow	Linn, Linne	Pool
		Meall	Rounded hill
Cailleach	Old woman, hag	Monadh	Mountain
Camas	Channel, bay	Mor, Mhor	Large
Caol (as) (pron. Cool)	Sound, strait	Muc	Pig
		Ob, Oban	Bay
Cille (pron. Keel)	Church, cemetery	Poll, Phuill	Pool
		Reamhar	Thick
Creag	Cliff	Ron, Roinn	Seal
Cumhainn	Narrows	Ruadh	Red
Dearg	Red	Rubha	Headland
Doirlinn	Neck of land, beach	Sgeir	Rocky shoal
		Sgurr	Rocky peak
Dun	Castle, fort	Stac	Pinnacle
Dubh	Black	Sruth	Current
Eilean(an)	Island(s)	Tarbert	Narrow isthmus
Gabhar, Gobhair	Goat	Tigh	House
		Traigh	Sandy beach
Gamhainn	Calf	Uamh(a)	Cape
Garbh	Rough	Uig	Bay
Geal, Gheal	White		

Notes and Corrections

Index

The system adopted throughout the book has been to reproduce the spelling of place names used by the Hydrographic Department on the latest Admiralty charts. Users should be aware, however, that the word Mor (large, great) is also frequently spelt Mhor, for reasons incomprehensible to a mere sassenach (sassunach!). This also applies to Beg (Beag), but here the alphabet displacement is less bothersome. As other sources may adopt other spellings, it is therefore always worth checking the alternative spelling if the name cannot be found: the Admiralty have changed spellings in the past, and may do so again.

Place names beginning with a generic term (e.g. Eilean, Loch or Rubha) are indexed under their individual name. The numerous identical names – I would guess that there are several hundred Eilean Dubhs in Scotland – have been identified by a major feature – island or waterway – near or in which they lie.

Pages whose numbers are given in italics include a plan of the place indexed.